PosterAnnual2000

PosterAnnual2000

The International Annual of Poster Art
Das internationale Jahrbuch der Plakakunst
Le répertoire international de l'art de l'affiche

Creative Director: B. Martin Pedersen

Editors: Heinke Jenssen, Phil Presby, Jamie Reynolds

Art Director: Lauren Slutsky

Photographer: Alfredo Parraga

Published by Graphis Inc.

Dedicated to Herbert Leupin (1916-1999)

ContentsInhaltSommaire

Remarks: We extend our heartfelt thanks to contributors throughout the world who have made it possible to publish a wide and international spectrum of the best work in this field. Entry instructions for all Graphis books may be requested at www.graphis.com.

Anmerkungen: Unser Dank gilt den Einsendern aus aller Welt, die es uns ermöglicht haben, ein breites, internationales Spektrum der besten Arbeiten zu veröffentlichen. Teilnahmebedingungen für die Graphis-Bücher sind erhältlich unter: www.graphis.com.

Remerciements: Nous remercions les participants du monde entier qui ont rendu possible la publication de cet ouvrage offrant un panorama complet des meilleurs travaux. Les modalités d'inscription peuvent être obtenues auprès de www.graphis.com.

(Opposite page) A poster for Center for the Arts, designed by Hui-Ling Chen of the Academy of Art College

(*Opposite page*) A poster for Cirque de Soleil, designed by Su Lee of Academy of Art College

THE WONDERFUL WORLD OF

Catskill Cuisine

Sept 21st   12 to 3 pm

AT WINDOWS ON THE WORLD 106TH FLOOR BALLROOM B HOSTED BY MICHAEL LOMONACO

A FANTASTIC MARKETPLACE TASTING OF THE BOUNTIFUL CATSKILL HARVEST

MEET THE FARMERS!

MEET THE CHEFS!

MARIO BATALI OF BABBO
ALEX LEE OF RESTAURANT DANIEL
TOM COLICCHIO OF GRAMERCY TAVERN
JOSH EDEN OF JEAN GEORGES
DAVID BOULEY OF RESTAURANT BOULEY
LEE HANSON OF BALTHAZAR
BILL TELEPAN OF JUDSON GRILL
ERIC MANN AND HEATHER HAVILAND OF THE BEAR CAFE
DAN BARBER OF DAN BARBER CATERING
WALDY MALOUF OF BEACON

TASTE THE MAGIC!
FINGERLING POTATOES
GERMAN BUTTERBALLS
BUTTERNUT SQUASH
QUAIL EGGS
ORGANIC VEAL
SHELL BEANS SHALLOTS
BEETS
MICRO GREENS
RABBIT
FOIE GRAS
MAPLE SYRUP
DUCK
PASTURED POULTRY
BROOK TROUT
GOAT CHEESE
CHARENTAIS MELONS
LAMB

BY INVITATION ONLY

SPONSORED BY
THE CATSKILL CENTER FOR CONSERVATION AND DEVELOPMENT
THE WATERSHED AGRICULTURAL COUNCIL
CATS (CATSKILL ASSOC OF TOURISM SERVICES)
CATSKILL FAMILY FARMS

Milton Glaser

Stephan Bundi:
The Power of the Hand in the Age of
the Computer: The Poster

It seems that any discussion of graphic design must touch on the subject of computer technology, the impact it has had on design and reproduction techniques, and the way it has changed visual communication. This technology has also had a social impact: designers, for the most part, can no longer work in isolation from the technological developments occurring around them. Rather, designers, like members of just about every other profession, have come to rely on computers, peripheral devices and software. Although this relationship to new and ever-changing technology significantly boosts designers' productivity, it also puts them at the mercy of the hardware and software manufacturers and developers, and makes full networking with customers and suppliers an absolute necessity. Universal availability is having a major impact on the designer's rhythm of work and creative output. Computers have given graphic designers new possibilities for creating playful, sophisticated typography. Unfortunately legibility often suffers as a result. Electronic manipulation techniques have spawned new, unfamiliar visual worlds. We now sometimes see highly specialized advertising agencies and studios combining textual and visual messages to create posters which both provide information and can be enjoyed as works of art. On the whole, the visual language used in these posters relies heavily on graphic, typographic and photographic elements. Figurative elements in the form of drawn or painted illustrations are seldom, if ever, used. Despite the awesome power of this new technology, some designers still choose to do without it. They reserve their computer for office work or, at most, for the pre-printing stage. These few stalwarts prefer to hone their drawing and painting skills, the basic tools of their trade, combining them with a flair for visual communication. The result is surprising, striking images.

The work of these designers is to be found in *Graphis Posters*, a publication which for a quarter of a century has surveyed the whole world of poster design. Its pages have featured the works of the masters, graphic designers such as Paul Brühwiler, Seymour Chwast, Heinz Edelmann, Anke Feuchtenberger, Milton Glaser, Hans Hillmann, Claude Kuhn, Istvan Orosz, Lanny Sommese, Waldemar Swierzy, Franticek Starojewsky, Niklaus Troxler, Tomi Ungerer and Henning Wagenbreth. Typically, their creations appear in the most recent as well as the earliest editions. Demand for their work seems to have remained undiminished over the decades. Pixel technology offers no substitute for their unique signature and the way they interpret and represent the issues.

In the fine arts, drawing and painting appear to have been superseded or are only accepted as fringe activities. In contrast, for those of us in visual communications they still constitute a valid—and vibrant—form. Figurative representation, regardless of how abstract, is virtually a must when it comes to communicating clearly. Anyone who believes that figurative drawing is outmoded should ask whether designers will really have sufficient scope for putting across the message if they do without figurative representation altogether. Won't physiognomy in its broadest sense continue to fascinate? Can the current trend of ignoring the actual subject in favor of vague ciphers overlaid with difficult-to-read typographic elements outlast the fatigue that continual bouts with irony inspire?

A drawing is a creative work and interpretation rolled into one. It is not reproduction in a narrow sense, but always involves the representation of an idea, the tangible communication of a vision, using optical abstraction to bring content to life. A designer's work is driven and guided by an interplay of constants and variables: the object to be communicated and the knowledge of how it can be represented are the constants; the designer's personal touch and the element of chance and subjective interpretation are the variables. The more freely a designer works, the more clearly this process is reflected in the results. Honest communications designers always interpret the theme rather than themselves.

Despite the many different possibilities on offer, visual languages created by electronic means are often rather superficial and homogeneous. By contrast, hand-drawn representations, "imperfect" as they are, have a certain quality and charm which demand attention. The form and content of a hand-drawn or painted design can be so provocative that the poster remains imprinted on the viewer's memory simply because it stands out clearly on a billboard full of standard fare. If the viewer's curiosity is sufficiently aroused for them to go to the event or buy the product advertised, then the poster has done its job.

In a Schiller play for which I recently designed a poster, William Tell says that a strong man is strongest when he works alone. Designers who buck the trend by producing hand-drawn or painted work have to be strong, because their decisions cannot be easily rationalized. They cannot constantly call up their work on screen and reorganize it, so delegating to other people is seldom possible. To a certain extent they have to be totally and personally involved in a project, from the first sketches to the reproduction stage. Working alone can make a designer feel isolated and insecure—but can also bring euphoria and great contentment.

Stephan Bundi was born in Trun, Switzerland in 1950. After an apprenticeship with Young & Rubicam, he studied book design at the Academy of Fine Arts in Stuttgart, Germany. In 1975, he set up his own studio, doing book design, magazine design and, above all, posters. He has received numerous awards for his work, has exhibited it at museums and galleries worldwide, and has had pieces selected for the permanent design collections of the Museum of Modern Art (New York), the Musée de la Publicité (Paris) and the Museum für Preussischen Kulturbesitz (Berlin). His design interests extend to all styles and techniques including the computer. He teaches illustration at the Hochschule für Gestaltung (Design Academy) in Berne, Switzerland.

(Previous spread, left page)
Design Firm: Milton Glaser Inc.
Illustrator: Milton Glaser
Client: Watershed Agricultural Concil
Poster

**PEACE
A HUMAN
RIGHT
HAGUE APPEAL
FOR PEACE
MAY 11-15, 1999
THE HAGUE**
OFFICE 777 UN PLAZA
NEW YORK, NY 10017
TEL: 212 687 2623
hap99@igc.apc.org
www.haguepeace.org
or, c/o IALANA, Anna
Paulownastraat 103,
2518 BC The Hague,
THE NETHERLANDS
tel +31 70 363 4484
ialana@antenna.nl

(This page)
Design Firm: The Pushpin Group Inc
Illustrator: Seymour Chwast
Client: The Hague Appeal for Peace
Poster/Announcement

(This page)
Design Firm: Milton Glaser Inc.
Illustrator: Milton Glaser
Client: Theatre For A New Audience
Poster/ Announcement

(Opposite page)
Design Firm: Milton Glaser Inc.
Illustrator: Milton Glaser
Client: The Highschool of Music and Art
Poster

The art of teaching is only the art of awakening

The High School of Music and Art
60th Anniversary

This commemorative poster was conceived and created by Milton Glaser, (Music & Art '47) for the Alumni and Friends of LaGuardia High School of Music & Art and Performing Arts, NYC. Proceeds will benefit students currently at the school.

Milton Glaser

Das Plakat im Zeitalter des Computers
von Stephan Bundi

Wenn heute von Graphic Design die Rede ist, scheint es unumgänglich zu sein, die Computertechnologie zu erwähnen und die dadurch—sowohl in gestalterischer als auch in reproduktionstechnischer Hinsicht—veränderte Bildsprache. Aber auch auf das sozial veränderte Umfeld wird hingewiesen, der Gestalter ist nicht mehr allein und unabhängig, sondern an Computer und Peripheriegeräte gebunden. Das steigert zwar seine Produktivität ungemein, macht ihn aber auch abhängig von einer komplexen Technologie, von Hard- und Softwareherstellern, denen er ausgesetzt, von Kunden und Lieferanten, mit denen er vernetzt ist. Die ungehinderte gegenseitige Erreichbarkeit bestimmt seinen Arbeitsrhythmus, sein Schaffen.

In gestalterischer Hinsicht ist eine verspielte, vielschichtige Typographie—leider oft auf Kosten der Lesbarkeit—möglich geworden. Die elektronische Bildmanipulation lässt neue, unbekannte Bildwelten entstehen. Manchmal schaffen hoch spezialisierte Werbeagenturen und Studios mittels Text- und Bildinformationen Gesamtkunstwerke; in solchen Fällen kann ein Plakat als Information oder Unterhaltung genussvoll erlebt werden. Insgesamt bedeutet diese Bildsprache eine Hinwendung zum Graphischen, Typographischen und Photographischen, das Figurative als gezeichnete oder gemalte Illustration scheint in diesem Umfeld nicht oder nur noch selten eingesetzt zu werden.

Da gibt es aber noch immer die Einzelkämpfer und -kämpferinnen, die gestaltungstechnologische Möglichkeiten nicht nutzen und den Computer vielleicht für die Büroarbeit, bestenfalls für die Druckvorstufe einsetzen. Diese Gestalter entwickeln ihr ursprünglich erlerntes zeichnerisch-malerisches Handwerk unentwegt weiter und nutzen ihre visuelle Kommunikationsfähigkeit, um überraschende und treffende Bilder zu schaffen.

Ihre Namen finden wir im Graphis Poster Annual, das seit über einem Vierteljahrhundert einen Überblick über das weltweite Plakatschaffen gibt. In diesen Jahrbüchern sind die grossen zeichnenden und malenden Graphiker, sofern das altersmässig möglich ist, über Jahrzehnte hinweg vertreten: Paul Brühwiler, Seymour Chwast, Heinz Edelmann, Anke Feuchtenberger, Milton Glaser, Hans Hillmann, Claude Kuhn, Istvan Orosz, Lanny Sommese, Waldemar Swierzy, Franticek Starojewsky, Niklaus Troxler, Tomi Ungerer, Henning Wagenbreth und andere. Die Nachfrage nach ihren Arbeiten scheint unvermindert gross zu sein. Die persönliche Handschrift und die Denkweise, mit der Themen behandelt und umgesetzt werden, sind offenbar nicht durch Pixeltechnologie zu ersetzen.

Während in der freien Kunst Zeichnung und Malerei überholt oder nur als eine Möglichkeit am Rande akzeptiert zu sein scheinen, sind sie in der visuellen Kommunikation nach wie vor eine gültige Form der Mitteilung. Die figürliche Darstellung, egal in welchem Abstraktionsgrad, ist für die Verständlichkeit der Kommunikation geradezu Bedingung. Nur uns bekannte Zeichen und Chiffren können gelesen, übersetzt werden. Wer der Ansicht ist, die figürliche Zeichnung sei überholt, müsste sich fragen: Hat der gestaltende Mensch für alle Zukunft genügend Spielraum für seine Mitteilungen, wenn er vollkommen auf das Figurative verzichtet? Wird ihn das Physiognomische im weitesten Sinn nicht doch beschäftigen? Bewegt man sich heute wirklich noch auf einer diskutablen Stufe, wenn man den Gegenstand ausklammert und diffuse Chiffren, überlagert mit schwer lesbaren Elementen produziert?

Eine Zeichnung ist gleichzeitig Projekt und Interpretation. Sie ist keine Wiedergabe im engen Sinn, sie ist immer das Zeichen einer Idee, die sichtbare Mitteilung einer Vision, wobei sie in der optischen Abstraktion einen konkreten Inhalt bekommen kann. Ein Objekt und das Wissen, wie dieses zeichnerisch umgesetzt werden kann, als Konstante, die Handschrift, das Zufällige, subjektiv Interpretierte als Variable, lenken und treiben die schöpferische Arbeit voran. Je freier wir gestalten, desto deutlicher findet dieses Vorgehen Ausdruck im Resultat. Dabei wird der redliche Kommunikationsdesigner immer das Thema interpretieren und nicht sich selbst.

Die elektronisch geschaffene Bildsprache hat trotz der reichen Auswahl an Darstellungsmöglichkeiten oft etwas Glattes, Stereotypes. Die von einer zeichnenden Persönlichkeit geprägte Darstellung dagegen, das vergleichsweise Unperfekte erhält einen eigenen Reiz, eine eigene Qualität, weckt Aufmerksamkeit. Eine zeichnerisch-malerische Darstellung kann in Form und Inhalt so viel Provokation enthalten, dass sie in der Erinnerung haften bleibt, allein schon deshalb, weil sie das gewohnte Bild an den Plakatwänden unterbricht. Wenn anschliessend, als zweiter Schritt, beim Betrachter die Neugier auf das Produkt oder den Anlass geweckt wird, braucht dieser nur noch zu handeln, und der Werbeauftrag ist erfüllt.

«Der Starke ist am mächtigsten allein», sagt Schillers Wilhelm Tell in jenem Schauspiel, für das ich letzthin ein Plakat gestalten durfte. Der Zeichner als Einzelkämpfer muss zwangsläufig stark sein, denn seine Entscheidungen lassen sich nicht leicht rationalisieren, er kann seine Einfälle nicht immer abrufen und planen, deshalb kann er seine Arbeiten selten delegieren. Er steckt gewissermassen mit persönlichem Einsatz bis zum Hals in einer Sache, und zwar von der ersten Skizze bis zur Reproduktionsreife. Ein Werk allein zu schaffen, ohne elektronische Hilfsmittel und Mitarbeiter, kann hart sein. Aber auch sehr befriedigend.

Stephan Bundi wurde 1950 in Trun in der Schweiz geboren. Nach einer Graphikerlehre in der Agentur Young & Rubicam studierte er Buchgestaltung und Illustration an der Staatlichen Akademie der bildenden Künste in Stuttgart. 1975 gründete er sein Atelier in Bern und gestaltet seitdem Bücher, Zeitschriften und vor allem Plakate. Für seine graphische Arbeit erhielt er zahlreiche Auszeichnungen, er hat in Museen und Galerien in aller Welt ausgestellt und ist u.a. in den Sammlungen des Museum of Modern Art (New York), des Musée de la Publicité (Paris) und des Museums für Preussischen Kulturbesitz (Berlin) vertreten. Er interessiert sich für die unterschiedlichsten Darstellungstechniken, einschliesslich des Computers, und ist Dozent für Illustration an der Hochschule für Gestaltung in Bern.

L'affiche à l'ère de l'ordinateur
par Stephan Bundi

Actuellement, lorsque l'on parle de design graphique, on est presque obligé d'évoquer les progrès de l'informatique et l'impact qu'ils ont exercé sur le design, les techniques de reproduction et la communication visuelle dans son ensemble. Sans oublier les changements occasionnés au niveau social: aujourd'hui, le designer n'opère plus tout seul dans son coin, il doit s'en remettre à l'ordinateur et aux unités périphériques. Si le progrès lui a permis d'augmenter sa productivité, il l'a aussi rendu dépendant de technologies complexes, de fabricants de matériel et de logiciels, tout en l'obligeant à travailler en réseau avec ses clients et fournisseurs. Son rythme de travail et sa propension à créer reposent donc largement sur des échanges optimaux avec ses interlocuteurs.

Les ordinateurs permettent désormais de concevoir une typographie ludique et sophistiquée, souvent au détriment de la lisibilité et ouvrent la voie à la création de nouveaux mondes visuels. Ainsi, des agences de publicité hautement spécialisées parviennent à réunir texte et images de sorte à créer des affiches à la fois informatives et artistiques. Généralement, le langage visuel propre à ces affiches s'articule autour d'éléments graphiques, typographiques et photographiques. Les composantes figuratives peintes ou dessinées ne sont jamais ou que rarement utilisées dans ce contexte.

Il existe néanmoins toujours quelques rebelles farouchement opposés à ces nouvelles technologies, qui recourent peut-être à l'ordinateur pour des travaux administratifs ou, dans le meilleur des cas, pour la pré-impression. Ces designers réfractaires préfèrent perfectionner inlassablement leur capacité à peindre ou à dessiner, la base de leur métier, et combiner leur talent avec un sens aigu de la communication visuelle pour donner forme à des images saisissantes et surprenantes.

Graphis Poster Annual, vitrine internationale du monde de l'affiche depuis plus de 25 ans, accorde une large place aux travaux de ces designers hors norme. Parmi les maîtres du genre, qui occupent depuis toujours une place de choix dans les pages de cette publication, figurent, entre autres, Paul Brühwiler, Seymour Chwast, Heinz Edelmann, Anke Feuchtenberger, Milton Glaser, Hans Hillmann, Claude Kuhn, Istvan Orosz, Lanny Sommese, Waldemar Swierzy, Franticek Starojewsky, Niklaus Troxler, Tomi Ungerer et Henning Wagenbreth. Au cours des décennies, leurs réalisations n'ont en rien perdu de leur attrait, et c'est toujours avec le même plaisir qu'on les admire. Les pixels et autres technologies ne peuvent en aucun cas substituer la signature distinctive de ces virtuoses du genre et leur façon d'appréhender et de traduire un thème.

Tandis que le dessin et la peinture semblent dépassés ou sont condamnés à jouer les seconds rôles dans le domaine des beaux-arts, ils constituent toujours une forme essentielle dans le monde de la communication visuelle. Une représentation figurative, peu importe son degré d'abstraction, est indispensable lorsqu'il s'agit de véhiculer un message clair. Quiconque pense que le dessin figuratif est démodé devrait peut-être se poser les questions suivantes: les concepteurs auront-ils un champ d'action assez vaste pour communiquer efficacement à l'avenir s'ils renoncent aux éléments figuratifs? La physionomie, dans son sens le plus large, ne continuera-t-elle pas à exercer la même fascination? Pourra-t-on longtemps ignorer le thème central au profit de vagues symboles recouverts d'éléments typographiques obscurs?

Un dessin tient du processus créatif et livre en même temps une interprétation. Il ne se limite pas à une simple reproduction, il inclut toujours la représentation d'une idée, la transmission tangible d'une vision, en se servant de l'abstraction optique pour donner vie à un contenu concret. L'œuvre d'un designer résulte de l'interaction de constantes et de variables: l'idée à communiquer et les connaissances acquises sur le moyen de l'exprimer se rangent parmi les constantes; la signature distinctive du designer, la place laissée au hasard et à l'interprétation subjective constituent les variables. Plus un designer travaille librement, plus ces éléments se cristalliseront dans le résultat. Les designers scrupuleux interprètent le thème plutôt qu'eux-mêmes.

Malgré un spectre de possibilités quasi illimitées, le langage visuel résultant de moyens électroniques est souvent superficiel, voire stéréotypé. Un dessin, aussi imparfait soit-il, présente par contre une qualité et un attrait propres, qui ne manquent pas de susciter l'attention. Une affiche peinte ou dessinée, à la forme ou au contenu provocants, restera gravée dans les mémoires par le seul fait qu'elle se détachera des créations standard placardées sur un mur d'affichage. Si elle capte de surcroît l'attention du passant et que celui-ci se rendra à la manifestation annoncée ou achètera le produit, alors elle aura atteint son objectif.

Dans une pièce de Schiller, pour laquelle j'ai récemment réalisé une affiche, Guillaume Tell déclare qu'un homme est le plus fort lorsqu'il agit seul. Les designers qui produisent des affiches peintes ou dessinées se doivent d'être forts parce que leurs décisions ne se laissent pas facilement rationaliser. Ils ne peuvent pas télécharger d'un simple clic leur travail à l'écran et le réorganiser, ni même en déléguer certains aspects à d'autres personnes. Ils sont en quelque sorte engagés jusqu'au cou dans leur projet et ce, de la première esquisse jusqu'à la phase de reproduction. Réaliser un travail seul, sans recourir à des moyens électroniques, est certes exigeant, mais tellement gratifiant.

Stephan Bundi est né en 1950 à Trun, en Suisse. Après un apprentissage de graphiste dans l'agence Young & Rubicam, il a étudié la conception de livres et l'illustration à l'Académie des beaux-arts de Stuttgart. En 1975, il ouvrait son propre atelier à Berne et conçoit depuis lors des livres, des magazines et notamment des affiches. Il a reçu de nombreux prix pour ses travaux graphiques et a exposé ses créations dans les galeries et musées du monde entier, dont le Museum of Modern Art de New York, le Musée de la Publicité de Paris et le Museum für Preussischen Kulturbesitz de Berlin. Il s'intéresse à tous les styles et techniques de représentation. Stephan Bundi enseigne également l'illustration à la Hochschule für Gestaltung de Berne, Suisse.

PosterAnnual2000

PosterAnnual2000

(Below)
Design Firm: Jennifer Sterling Design
Creative Director, Art Director,
Designer, Illustrator: Jennifer Sterling
Client: Southern California Institute
of Architecture

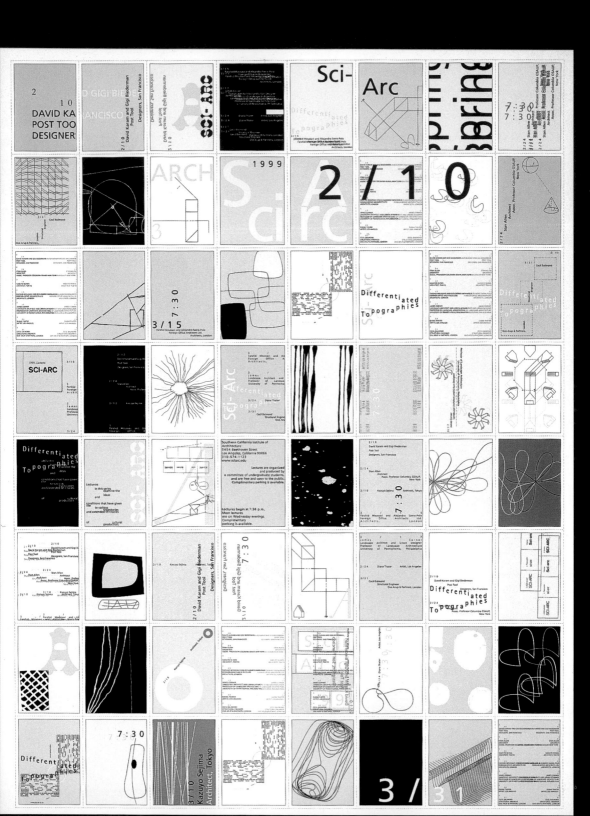

(Below)
Design Firm: Aufuldish & Warinner
Art Director, Designer, Photographer: Bob
Aufuldish
Çlient: Colorado AIGA

the house of brick could not be blown down

(This spread)
Design Firm: BBI Studio INC
Art Director, Designers: Zempaku Suzuki,
Hiroshi Yano
Writer: Nob Ogasawara
Photographer: Hiroshi Yoda

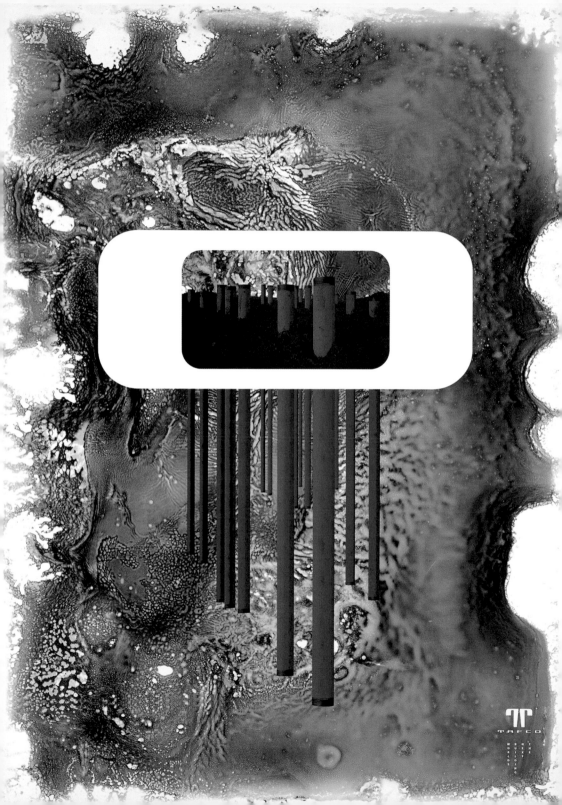

(This page)
Design Firm: The Martin Agency
Creative Directors: Kerry Feuerman,
Rob Shapiro
Art Directors: Noel Ritter, Jonathan
Mackler
Copywriter: Kerry Feuerman
Photographer: Clint Clemens
Client: Saab

(This page)
Design Firm: Lipson Alport
Glass & Associates
Art Director: Sam Ciulla,
Jim Pietruzynski
Photographer: Jim Pietruzynski
Client: Brand Design Association

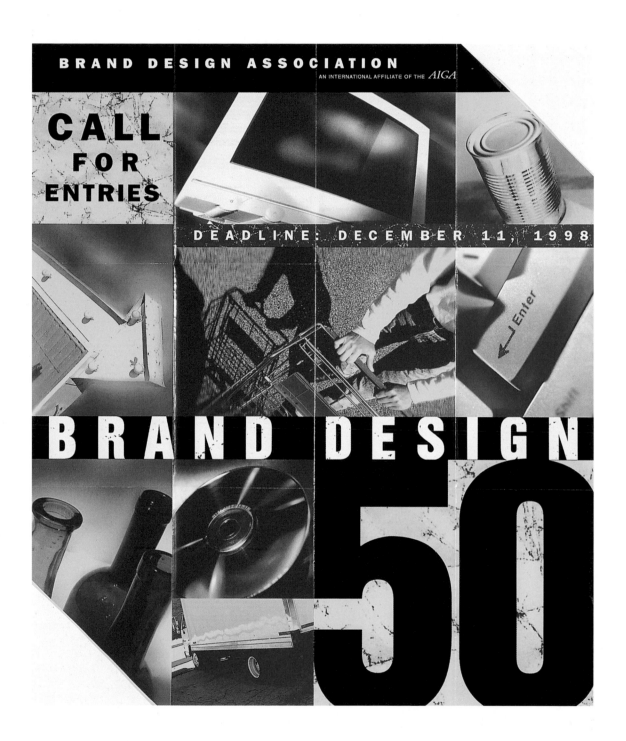

DALLAS SOCIETY OF VISUAL COMMUNICATIONS

★ presents the ★

1999 STUDENT COMPETITION

featuring the STUDENT SEMINAR, AGENCY TOUR and JOB FAIR

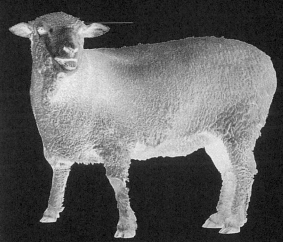

ORDER: ARTIODACTYLA / GENUS: OVIS
Control Specimen 23-b

"There Really is No Substitute for Being Original."

Hurry! Entry Deadline **March 19!**

(This page)
Creative Director, Designer: Ted Fabella
Client: AIGA Atlanta

(Opposite page)
Design Firm: Elan Communications
Creative Director, Art Director: Michael
Lorenero
Designer: Ying Ying Wong
Writer: Michael Lorenero
Illustrator: Michael Lorenero
Client: AIGA Pittsburgh Chapter

(This page)
Design Firm: Cole & Weber/Portland
Creative Director: Michael Nalley
Art Director: Sharon Barrett

Writer: Hart Rusen
Photographer: Lars Topelmann
Client: Visio Software

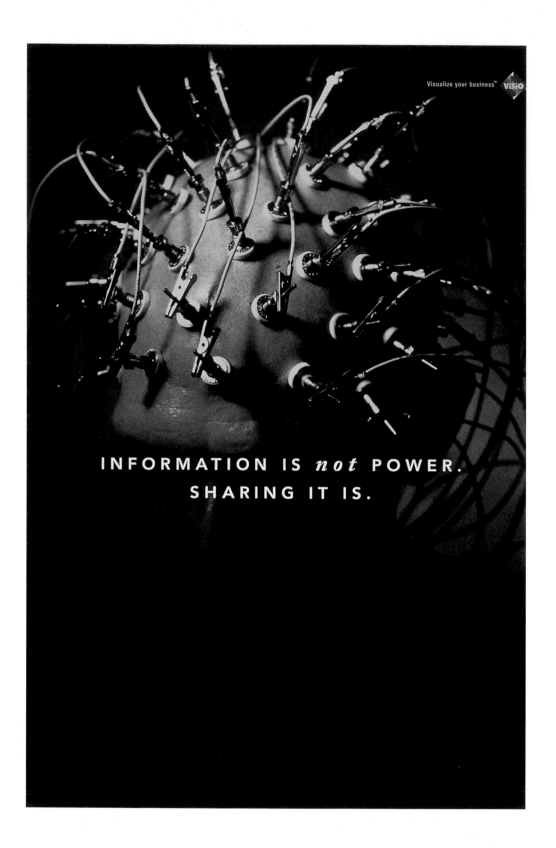

(Opposite page)
Design Firm: US Webicks
Creative Director: Andy Dreyfus
Art Director: Hiroki Asai
Photographer: Hunter Freeman
Client: Apple Computer

Yum.

Think different.

CSE/WORKFLOW®

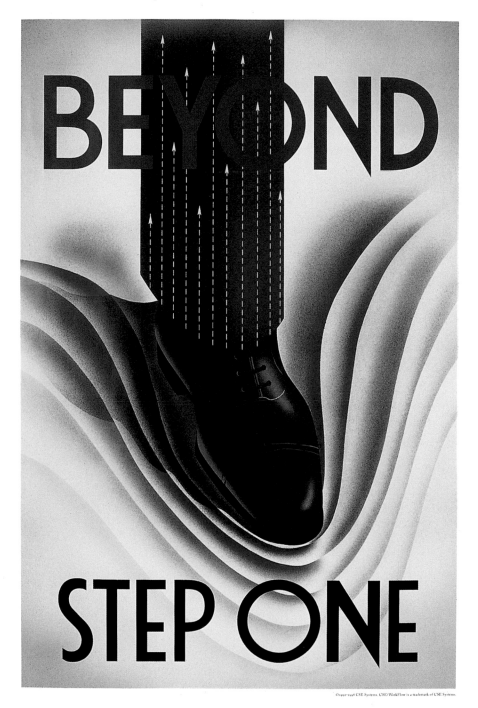

(This page)
Design Firm: RBMM
Creative Director: Dick Mtichell
Designer, Writer: James Starr

Photographer: John Lund
Client: EDS

Perhaps

YOUR COMPETITION'S *not* GIVING

YEAR 2000

THEIR *full* ATTENTION.

(But let's not rush to CORRECT THEM just yet.)

STILL, YOU MAY SENSE SERIOUS ISSUES looming on your own horizon, despite your progress in efforts to comply. We can help. ➤ EDS has already completed Y2K assignments ahead of schedule for many clients. And as you read this, a team of more than 1,000 EDS professionals, dedicated solely to Y2K, is preparing yet another for this historic milestone. ➤ For more information about how we can help you get on the train (instead of in front of it), please contact us at www.eds.com/y2k/   **EDS**

(Opposite page)
Creative Director, Art Director,
Designer: Tadanori Yokoo
Client: Hikawa-Jinta

Rooms for Improvement. Here's an offer that should sit well with you. At TCI we think you should be able to enjoy cable TV anywhere in your house. That's why TCI offers free or low cost additional outlets. Having cable on all of your TVs makes a real difference in your home entertainment. **A difference you can see.**

TCI

(Opposite page)
Design Firm: Vaughn Wedeen Creative
Creative Director, Art Director,
Designer: Steve Wedeen

Writer: Foste Hurley
Client: TCI

I W A S A K I

(This page)
Design Firm: Shin Matsunaga
Design Inc.
Creative Director, Art Director,
Designer: Shin Matsunaga
Client: Iwasaki Electric Co Ltd

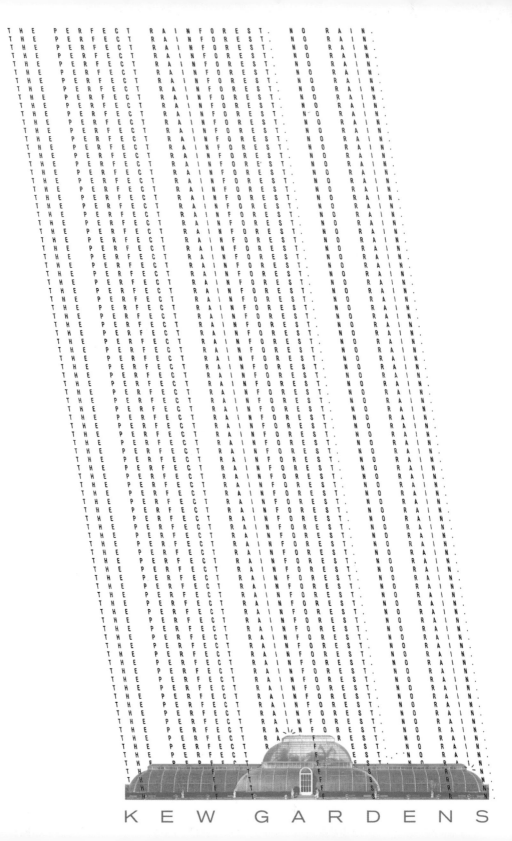

KEW GARDENS

(This page)
Design Firm: Ogilvy One
Creative Director: Bruce Lee
Art Director: Marcelo Guidoli
Designer: Marcelo Guidoli,

Cynthia Dauzie
Writer: Bruce Lee
Illustrator: Marcelo Guidoli
Client: Ogilvy One

Use it wisely.

Resume to: ogilvyone.com

(Opposite page)
Design Firm: TBWA GGT
Simons Palmer
Creative Director: Trevor Beattie

Art Director, Designer: Paul Belford
Writer: Nigel Roberts
Client: Kew Gardens

(This page)
Design Firm: Graphica Inc
Creative Director: Mark Stockstill
Art Director, Designer:
Drew Cronenwett
Client: IBM Global Channel Marketing

(Opposite page)
Creative Director, Art Director,
Designer, Photographer: Bing-Wah
Client: Shanghai Grand Sunfire
Property Development Co

(This page)
Designer: Su Lee
School: Academy of Art College
Client: Cirque de Soleil

the *VALENTINE* festival

Rubies - Stravinsky/Balanchine
Beyond Innocence - World Premiere Enigma/Morgan
Con Amore - Rossini/Christensen

Aronoff Center for the Arts
Friday, February 12 at 8 p.m.
Saturday, February 13 at 2 p.m. & 8 p.m.
Tickets: Aronoff Center Box Office
Ticketmaster 513-241-SHOW
Group Rates 513-621-5219 ext.114

the *SLEEPING BEAUTY*

Company Premiere Tchaikovsky/Poole

Aronoff Center for the Arts
Friday, March 19 at 8 p.m.
Saturday, March 20 at 2 p.m. & 8 p.m.
Sunday, March 21 at 2 p.m.
Tickets: Aronoff Center Box Office
Ticketmaster 513-241-SHOW
Group Rates 513-621-5219 ext. 114

 BUTTERFLY

Company Premiere **Puccini/Nixon**

Aronoff Center for the Arts
Friday, April 23 at 8 p.m.
Saturday, April 24 at 2 p.m. & 8 p.m.
Sunday, April 25 at 2 p.m.
Tickets: Aronoff Center Box Office
Ticketmaster 513-241-SHOW
Group Rates 513-621-5219 ext. 114

season sponsored by
CINERGY.
FOUNDATION

Butterfly sponsored by ♦ KeyBank

CINCINNATI
Ballet
Victoria Morgan, Artistic Director
Carmon DeLeone, Music Director

PRACTICE.
PRACTICE.
PRACTICE.
PRACTICE.
PRACTICE.
PERFORM.
PRACTICE.
PRACTICE.
PRACTICE.
PRACTICE.

Boston Ballet

41 PEOPLE DIDN'T

BECOME BANKERS.

OR LAWYERS.

OR ENGINEERS.

OR BROKERS.

OR ACCOUNTANTS

Boston Ballet

(This page)
Design Firm: Cyclone
Designer: Dennis Clouse, Traci Daberko

FUNNEL
TWISTER
TORNADO
TYPHOON
CYCLONE

WHEN WRITTEN IN CHINESE, THE WORD CRISIS IS COMPOSED OF TWO CHARACTERS. ONE REPRESENTS DANGER AND THE OTHER REPRESENTS OPPORTUNITY.

CYCLONE DESIGN & ILLUSTRATION · 206-323-7357

(This page)
Design Firm: Sagmeister Inc
Creative Director, Art Director,
Designer: Stefan Sagmeister

Illustrator: Martin Woodtli
Photographer: Tom Schierlitz
Client: AIGA Detroit

Designers 46, 47

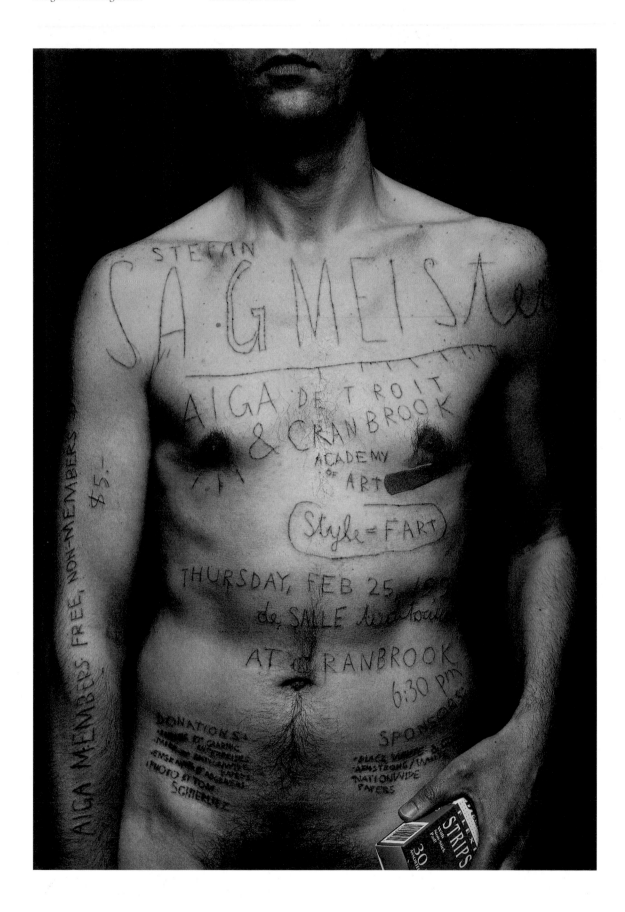

(This page)
Design Firm: Sagmeister Inc
Creative Director, Art Director,
Designer: Stefan Sagmeister

Illustrator: Martin Woodtli
Photographer: Tom Schierlitz
Client: AIGA Detroit

(This spread, next spread)
Design Firm: Art Force Studio
Creative Director: Simon Attila
Art Director, Designer: Veress Tamas
Illustrator: Veress Tamas
Client: Art Force Studio

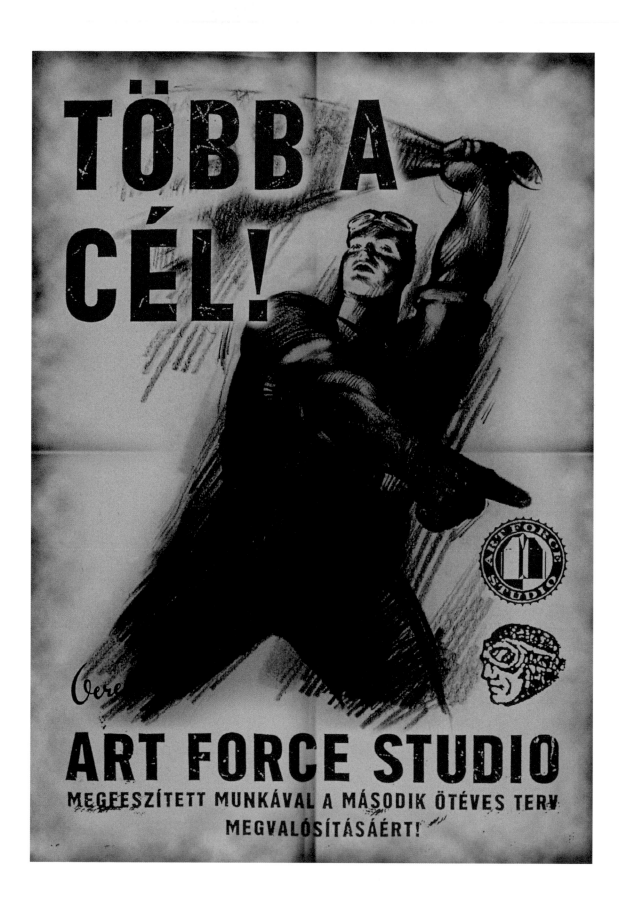

Én is az *Art Force* Studioval utazom!

GRAFIKAI PARÁDÉ
AZ ART FORCE STUDIOBAN
MINDENNAP 9-18 ÓRÁIG

(This page)
Design Firm: Balance Design

(Opposite page)
Design Firm: Shin Matsunaga
Design Inc
Creative Director, Art Director,
Designer: Shin Matsunaga
Photographer: Shin Matsunaga
Client: Japan Graphic Designers
Association Inc

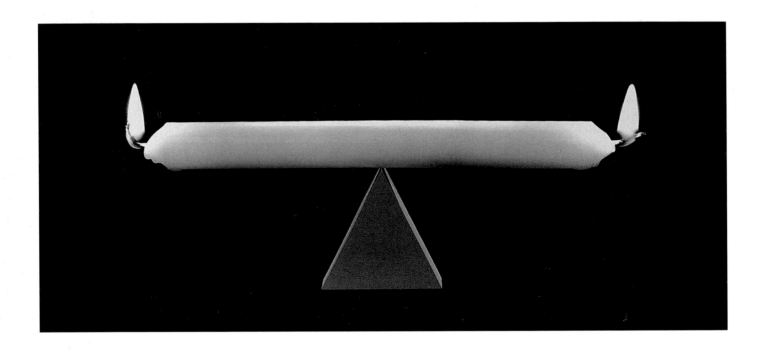

(Next spread)
Design Firm: Maksimovic & Partners
Art Director: Imaksimovic,
Patrick Bittner
Designer: Patrick Bittner, Isabel Bach
Writer Patrick Bittner
Photographer: Natascha Maksimovic
Client: Versorgungs-Und
Verkehrsgesellschaft SAA
Citylights 1 S B

D E S I G N

Eine tausendjährige Stadt in anderem Licht. Die Versorgungs- und Verkehrsgesellschaft Saarbrücken schenkt Saarbrücken zum Jubiläum neue Einsichten und Ansichten. In Form von Licht. Klang. Kunst und Gedanken. Vom 4. bis zum 6. Juni 1999. Beim Symposion »Highlights – Von der Erleuchtung über die Lichtgeschwindigkeit zur Lightshow«.

l.s.b.
– licht. saar. brücken.

3 Tage | mehr Licht

Die VVS.

> 04.06. 18.00 – 19.00 Uhr Paul Virilio Vortrag »Lichtgeschwindigkeit« im Haus der Zukunft 22.00 Uhr Filmvorführung »Der Strom« beim Heizkraftwerk Römerbrücke 05.06. 9.30 Uhr Filmvorführung »The Passageway« im Großen Sitzungszimmer der Stadtwerke 11.00 Uhr Friedrich Kittler Vortrag im Heizkraftwerk Römerbrücke 12.30 Uhr Peter Bexte Vortrag »Blinde Optiker« während der Fahrt mit der Saarbahn nach Sarreguemines 17.00 Uhr Wolfgang Hagen Vortrag »Funken und Scheinbilder« in der Werkstatt der Saartal-Linien 18.30 – 19.30 Uhr Hanns Zischler Lesung »Text über die Elektrizität« im Lager Weyerbachtal 22.00 Uhr John Cage Videopräsentation »one[11] + 103« in Messehalle 6 23.00 Uhr DJ Dr. Motte Disco und Lightshow in Messehalle 1 06.06. 10.00 – 11.30 Uhr Filmvorführung »Der Pfad der Erleuchtung« im Filmhaus 12.00 – 13.00 Uhr Peter Weibel Vortrag »Bild-Licht« im Haus der Zukunft. <

→ DER EINTRITT ZU ALLEN VERANSTALTUNGEN IST FREI. [Infos unter Telefon: 0681-587 24 81 | e-mail: info@vvs-konzern.de]

l.s.b.
- licht. saar. brücken.

Drei Tage mehr Licht

Eine tausendjährige Stadt in anderem Licht. Die Versorgungs- und Verkehrsgesellschaft Saarbrücken schenkt Saarbrücken zum Jubiläum neue Einsichten und Ansichten. In Form von Licht. Klang, Kunst und Gedanken. Vom 4. bis zum 6. Juni 1999. Beim Symposion »Highlights — Von der Erleuchtung über die Lichtgeschwindigkeit zur Lightshow«

[Infos unter Telefon: 0681-587 24 81 | e-mail: info@vvs-konzern.de]

> 04.06. 18.00 - 19.00 Uhr Paul Virilio Vortrag »Lichtgeschwindigkeit« im Haus der Zukunft 22.00 Uhr Filmvorführung »Der Strom« beim Heizkraftwerk Römerbrücke 05.06. 9.30 Uhr Filmvorführung »The Passageway« im Großen Sitzungszimmer der Stadtwerke 11.00 Uhr Friedrich Kittler Vortrag im Heizkraftwerk Römerbrücke 12.30 Uhr Peter Bexte Vortrag »Blinde Optiker« während der Fahrt mit der Saarbahn nach Sarreguemines 17.00 Uhr Wolfgang Hagen Vortrag »Funken und Scheinbilder« in der Werkstatt der Saartal-Linien 18.30 - 19.30 Uhr Hanns Zischler Lesung »Text über die Elektrizität« im Lager Weyerbachtal 22.00 Uhr John Cage Videopräsentation »one^{11} + 103« in Messehalle 6 23.00 Uhr DJ Dr. Motte Disco und Lightshow in Messehalle 1 06.06. 10.00 - 11.30 Uhr Filmvorführung »Der Pfad der Erleuchtung« im Filmhaus 12.00 - 13.00 Uhr Peter Weibel Vortrag »Bild-Licht« im Haus der Zukunft. <

→ DER EINTRITT ZU ALLEN VERANSTALTUNGEN IST FREI. Die VVS.

(This spread)
Design Firm: BBI Studio Inc
Art Director: Zempaku Suzuki
Designer: Yohko Fujita

Writer: Nob Ogasawara
Client: BBI Studio Inc

Evolution; it is the instant

in which the cells of design

metamorphose for survival.

It is as if they have a survival instinct

that hints at the creation of the world.

That is how it feels.

BBI STUDIO
PROCREATION PERIOD

fusion: it is the instant

in which the cells of design

plant roots for staking their presence

it is as if our spirits are filled

with pleasure that burn like the sun

that is how it feels

BBI STUDIO
PROCREATION PERIOD

(This page)
Design Firm: Kan & Lau Design
Consultants
Creative Director, Art Director,

Designer: Kan Tai-Keung
Photographer: CK Wong
Client: *Communication Arts* magazine

Communication Arts

Special Feature on the work of Kan Tai-keung January/February 1999

御

製作＝大島渚プロダクション

法

GOHATTO

度

製作・配給＝松竹

Creative Director, Art Director,
Designer: Tadanori Yokoo
Client: Shochiku Co Ltd

Dein Körper ist kein Mann.
Du kannst nicht irgendwann ausziehen
und Dir einen attraktiveren suchen.

SHAPE

FÜR FRAUEN, DIE IN FORM SEIN WOLLEN.

Susanne, fotografiert von Susanne.

Was einen perfekten Körper ausmacht?
Eine Frau, die sagt: "Hier drin fühl ich mich wohl."

SHAPE

FÜR FRAUEN, DIE IN FORM SEIN WOLLEN.

Stefanie, fotografiert von Stefanie.

(This page)
Design Firm: Jager di Paola
Kemp Design
Creative Director: Michael Jager
Art Director: David Covell

Designer: David Covell, Denis Kegler
Writer: David Covell
Client: Jager di Paola Kemp Design

(This page)
Design Firm: Storm Image Design
& Development
Creative Directors: David Ansett,

Dean Butler
Designer: Michelle Gauci
Client: Photomanifesto

(This page)
Design Firm: Inpetho Medien
Produktion GMBH
Designer: Andreas Wallat
Client: Inpetho Medien
Produktion GMBH

互動 interaction

(This page)
Design Firm: *Graphic Communications*
Bimonthly
Creative Director, Art Director,
Designer: Wang Su-Chao

Writer: Wang Su-Chao
Illustrator: Wang Su-Chao
Client: Chinese Poster
Design Association

(This page)
Photographer: Earl Carter
Client: Swinburne School of Design

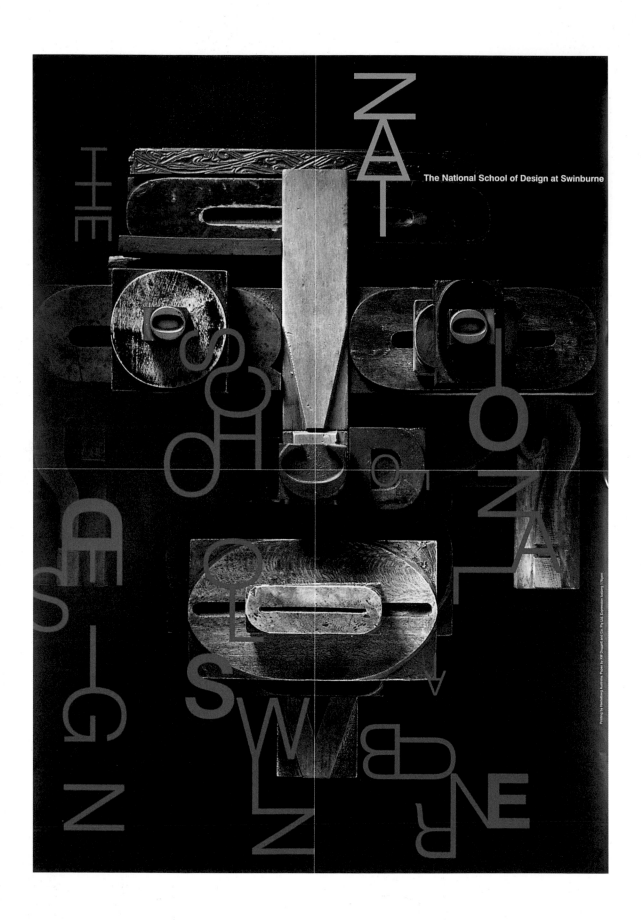

The National School of Design at Swinburne

(This page)
Photographer: Earl Carter
Client: Swinburne School of Design

(Opposite page)
Design Firm: Pentagram Design Inc
Art Director: Woody Pirtle

CHILDHOOD
IS NOT CHILD'S PLAY

STİL MATBAACILIK A.Ş.

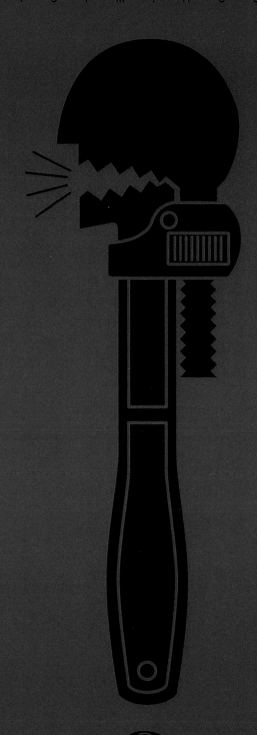

STİL MATBAACILIK A.Ş.

(This page)
Design Firm: Frank Baseman Design
Creative Director, Art Director,
Designer: Frank Baseman
Writer: Frank Baseman
Photographer: Frank Baseman
Client: Philadelphia CLG of Textile

SCHOOL OF architecture AND design

Architecture   Graphic Design   Industrial Design   Interior Design

Spring

fig. [a] spring

PHILADELPHIA COLLEGE OF TEXTILES & SCIENCE

For more information contact the School of Architecture and Design (215)951-2896 or www.philacol.edu

JANUARY 8, 6:00pm
IAN LIDDELL
Structural Engineer
Buro, Happold Engineers
London, England
"The Millennium Dome Project"
Media Room, Gutman Library
Sponsored by Fabric Architecture Magazine

MARCH 16, 6:00pm
URSULA DAYENIAN
Interior Designer
Legat Architects, Chicago
"Creative and Strategic Thinking in Interior Design"
Media Room, Gutman Library

MARCH 24, 6:00pm
CHIP KIDD
Graphic Designer/Art Director/Writer
Alfred A. Knopf Publishing Co., New York
Downs Hall
*Sponsored by The American Institute of Graphic Arts,
Philadelphia chapter and Potlatch Corporation*

APRIL 8, 6:00pm
ROBERT BLAICH
*Industrial Designer, Design Management
and Strategic Planning Consultant*
Aspen, Colorado
"Design Leadership"
Downs Hall
*Sponsored by the Industrial Design Society of America,
Philadelphia chapter*

APRIL 15, 6:00pm
DANIEL LIBESKIND
Architect
Daniel Libeskind and Nina Libeskind
Berlin, Germany
Downs Hall
*Sponsored by Francis Cauffman Foley Hoffmann
Architects, Philadelphia*

APRIL 21, 6:00pm
DAVID PISCUSKAS
Architect
1100 Architect, New York
David Piscuskas and Juergen Riehm, partners
Downs Hall
Sponsored by Vitetta Group

*Sponsored by Asten, Inc. as part of
the Dietrich Asten Global Awareness Project*

1999

spring *lecture* **SERIES**

DON'T MISS OUR EXTRAORDINARY TRANSFORMATION RIGHT BEFORE YOUR VERY EYES. WE'RE MORE AMAZING. MORE ASTOUNDING. AND WE'VE MOVED. COME WITNESS US AT OUR NEW LOCATION, HITHERTO THOUGHT AN IMPOSSIBLE FEAT. BEHOLD SPECTACULAR ARTISTIC PERFORMANCES EXECUTED WITH MARVELOUS GRACE, EASE AND PERFECTION. THRILL TO THE MOST REMARKABLE COLLECTION OF TALENT WORLDWIDE IN ONE PLACE. THE CREATIVE CIRCUS.

PAPER: JUDY LAUBER, OLMSTEAD-KIRK, AUSTIN / PRINTING: SHIRLEY RICHARDSON, WILLIAMSON PRINTING, DALLAS / CONCEPT & DESIGN: SIBLEY/PETEET DESIGN, AUSTIN   CREATIVE CIRCUS / 812 LAMBERT DRIVE N.E. / ATLANTA, GEORGIA 30324 / PH: 404.607.8880 / FAX: 404.875.1590 / TOLL-FREE: 800.728.1590 / WWW.CREATIVECIRCUS.COM

EXPOSE YOUR CREATIVE SIDE.

TEXAS A&M COMMERCE INVITES YOU TO THIS YEAR'S ART DAY AND PHOTO SHOOT OUT ON FEBRUARY 27, 1999.

IT'S A DAY WHEN OUR PROFESSORS LEAD SEMINARS INVOLVING CLAY, PAINT, CHEMICALS, LIGHT AND YOU.

IT'S A CHANCE TO DEVELOP YOUR SKILLS AND FOCUS YOUR MIND AT ONE OF THE FINEST ART SCHOOLS IN THE STATE.

WHO KNOWS, YOU MAY EVEN WIN A SCHOLARSHIP.

PRINTING GRACIOUSLY PROVIDED BY WILLIAMSON PRINTING, TEXAS, TEXAS

(*This page*)
Design Firm: Emerson
Wajdowicz Studios
Creative Director, Art Director:
Jurek Wajdowicz
Designer: L. Larochelle, Jurek Wajdowicz
Photographer: Victor Mello
Client: United Nations Office

(This spread)
Design Firm: yeh Design Co Ltd
Creative Director, Art Director,
Designer: Gary Yeh Kuo Sung
Writer: Gary Yeh Kuo Sun

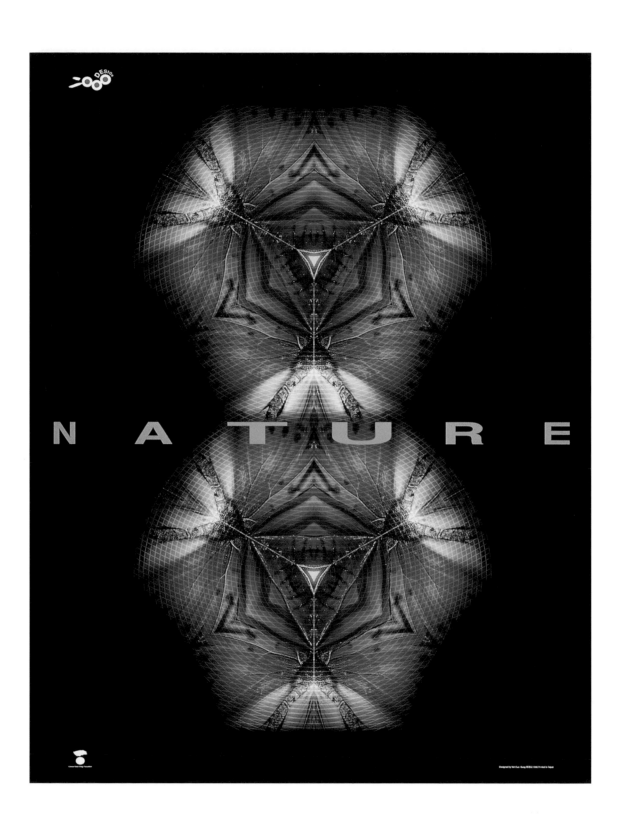

(This page)
Design Firm: Savas Cekic Tasarim
Creative Director, Art Director,
Designer: Savas Cekic
Illustrator: Savas Cekic
Client: Stil Print House

(This page)
Design Firm: Takashi Akityama Studio
Art Director, Designer: Takashi Akiyama
Illustrator: Takashi Akiyama
Client: Japan Campaign to
Ban Landmines

(Next Spread)
Art Director, Designer: Jim Ales
Writer: Mike Rigsby
Illustrator: Larry Duke
Client: Monterey Bay Aquarium
Monterey Bay Habitats

KELP FOREST

From its base on the rocks to its broad canopy above, a kelp forest provides food and shelter for rich communities of life. From their rocky anchors, giant kelp plants stretch upward to the sunlight, forming a thick carpet of fronds at the surface. Harbor seals and cormorants dive down from above to seek the bounty of the golden forest. Blue rockfish and schools of golden señoritas slip between the sheltering fronds. Top snails and kelp crabs graze on the living kelp while abalone, red and purple sea urchins and bat stars graze on detached fronds that drift to the forest floor. They in turn may fall prey to wolf-eels, lingcod and other, larger predators, like sea otters. Among the tangled holdfasts on the seafloor, strawberry sea anemones, cup corals and blue sponges compete for space and food.

MONTEREY BAY AQUARIUM®

ROCKY SHORE

Emerald tide pools teem with life along rocky, wave-swept coastlines. The rise and fall of the tides sets the patterns of life, creating distinct zones, each with its own community of plants and animals. At the upper reaches of the tides, limpets and periwinkles roam rocks splashed only occasionally by the sea. Though they cling tight, they may still fall prey to the prying bills of black oystercatchers. Lower down, where rockweeds carpet rocks submerged each day by high tides, ochre sea stars hunt goose barnacles and mussels. Here sea palms bob in the surging waves, while Turkish towel, feather boa kelp and narweed sway with the sea's motion. Still lower, where the sea claims the rocks much of the day, the kelp gardens grow more lush, and animals more abundant. A red octopus patrols a deep pool in search of a meal, perhaps a leather chiton or a decorator crab.

MONTEREY BAY AQUARIUM®

(This page)
Design Firm: Leslie Chan
Design Co Ltd
Creative Director, Art Director:
Leslie Chan Wing Kei
Designer: Leslie Chan Wing Kei,
Larcher Chao
Photographer: Larcher Chao
Client: Chinese Poster
Design Association

(This spread)
Design Firm: Emerson
Wajdowicz Studios
Creative Director, Art
Director: Jurek Wajdowicz
Designer: Lisa Larochelle,

Jurek Wajdowicz
Photographer: Victor Mello
Client: United Nations
Office for Project Services

Something's happening in

Bangui

Free and fair elections.
Parliamentary elections in the Central African Republic were organized in record time and garnered a 70% turnout with support from donors and the United Nations.

UNOPS
Managing forward.

Something's happening in

Sustainable harvests.
India's hill tribes are finding ways to get more
out of the land through an IFAD-funded project
supervised by UNOPS.

Vishakhapatnam

UNOPS
Managing forward.

(Opposite page)
Design Firm: Peterson & Company
Creative Director, Art Director,
Designer: Scott Ray
Writer: Dorit Suffness
Photographer: Doug Davis
Client: Dallas Society of Visual
Communication

(This spread)
Creative Director, Art Director,
Designer: Tadanori Yokoo
Client: Toppan Printing Co Ltd

(This page)
Design Firm: Pentagram Design Inc
Art Director: Michael Bierut
Designer: Nicole Trice
Client: Architectural League of New
York

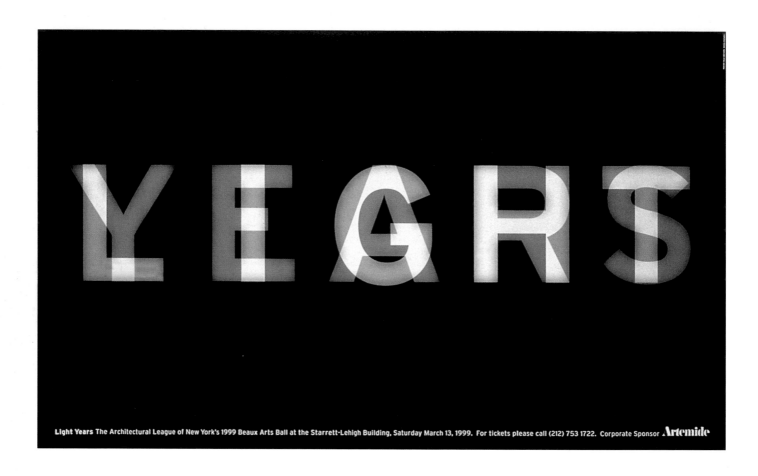

Light Years The Architectural League of New York's 1999 Beaux Arts Ball at the Starrett-Lehigh Building, Saturday March 13, 1999. For tickets please call (212) 753 1722. Corporate Sponsor Artemide

(Opposite page)
Design Firm: Daehong
Communication Inc
Creative Director, Art Director:
Hyun Tai Kim
Writer: Jae Hak Kim
Photographer: Kyu Hwan Pyo
Client: Daehong Communication Inc

Delicious Harmony

『Oullim, The Great Harmony』 1996 Created by Kim, Hyun Tai

(This spread)
Design Firm: GSD&M
Art Director, Designer: Fred
Huddleston, James Welsh
Writer: Fred Huddleston, James Welsh

Photographer: Andrew Yates
Client: Big Stinkin Intl Improv
& Sketch Comedy

Durham Fair 1998

THE SEVENTY-NINTH
CONNECTICUT'S
LARGEST
AGRICULTURAL
EXHIBITION
ANNUAL DURHAM FAIR

**The Seventy-Ninth
Annual Durham Fair**

**Connecticut's Largest
Agricultural Exhibition**

**September 25, 26, & 27,
Nineteen Ninety-Eight**

*The character of the
Durham Fair, like the
Hypolimnas Pandarus,
is always changing yet
always the same. The
collections and exhibits,
everything from arcades
to zucchini are all here.
Mixed with the sights
and sounds of happy
children and old
friends; The Durham
Fair.*

America : Cult & Culture We're open 24 Hours

A
I
QUE
PARKING
G
A

AIGA
in
Las Vegas

THE **AIGA's** (*8th*) BIENNIAL **NATIONAL DESIGN CONFERENCE**

THE VENETIAN HOTEL, LAS VEGAS SEPTEMBER 29-OCTOBER 2, 1999
TO REGISTER CALL [212] 807.1990 OR VISIT www.aiga.org

(This page)
Design Firm: Cahan & Associates
Creative Director, Art Director:
Bill Cahan
Designer: Kevin Roberson
Writer: Kevin Roberson

FLUORESCENT LIGHTING
SIX-FOOT SQUARE CUBICLE
LETTER-SIZE FILE DRAWER
SANITIZED LABCOAT
ONE-HOUR COMMUTE
EMPLOYEE BREAK ROOM
BOARD MEETING
FDA REGULATIONS

POTENTIAL CURE
FOR CANCER

CLIMATE CONTROL
OVERHEAD PROJECTOR
TRADE CONFERENCE
CLINICAL TRIAL DATA
PRESS RELEASE
PATENT APPLICATION

NON-SURGICAL
TREATMENT FOR
HEART DISEASE

AIGA/WICHITA & APPLETON PAPERS PRESENT

*MATTER

Bill Cahan of Cahan & Associates speaks on the challenges and opportunities of designing for the corporate arena. Many of the firm's clients work in design resistant industries such as pharmaceuticals, computer peripherals, and enterprise software solutions. At first glance, these companies appear to be anonymous formations of tilt-up architecture, climate controlled conference rooms and shredded legal documents. Their inhabitants may seem buried in the quagmire of scientific detail and mundane corporate duties. However, with a bit of excavation and a lot of exploring, it is quite possible to discover what really matters. / **Friday** May 28th 11:30am / **Sponsor** Appleton Papers / **Host** AIGA Wichita

CASUAL FRIDAY
EMPLOYEE NEWSLETTER
9 X 12 ENVELOPE
MARKETING MEETING
COMPANY RETREAT
RESEARCH CONFERENCE

CURE FOR
BLINDNESS IN
AIDS PATIENTS

ANALYST REPORT
SCIENCE JOURNAL ARTICLE
LEGAL-SIZE FILE DRAWER
UNIVERSITY PRESENTATION
HALF-HOUR COMMUTE
GENE THERAPY SEMINAR
NEW DRUG APPLICATION
STOCK VALUE

METHOD OF ENABLING
PEOPLE TO REMAIN
HEALTHY AS THEY AGE

EXCAVATIONS / EXPLORATIONS / EXECUTIVES

(This page)
Design Firm: Studio D Design
Art Director, Designer:
Laurie Demartino
Photographer: Aaron Dimmel
Client: Art Directors Association of Iowa

(Opposite page)
Design Firm: 30 Sixty Design Inc
Creative Director: Henry Vizcarra

(Opposite page)
Creative Director, Designer:
Ted Fabella
Client: ADMP

Beg, Borrow, or Steal?

(This page)
Design Firm: Sibley Peteet Design
Creative Director, Art Director,
Designer: David Beck
Writer: Duane Michals

Photographer: Duane Michals
Client: Dallas Society
of Visual Communication

01

Izložba hrvatskog dizajna
Exhibition of Croatian design
GF Galerija Forum
Teslina 16, Zagreb
08.04. - 20.04. 1999.
Organizator / Organiser:
Hrvatsko dizajnersko društvo
Suorganizator / Coorganiser:
KIC Kulturno informativni centar
Izlažu / Exhibits by:
Mihajlo Arsovski
Iva Babaja
Ana Baletić
Marko Baus
Ian Borčić
Vanessa Borčić
Željko Borčić
Stipe Brčić
Davor Bruketa
Raul Brzić
Rajna Buzić Ljubičić
Lana Cavar
Nenad Dogan
Ivan Doroghy
Dejan Dragosavac-Rutta
Dražen Đuroković
Marijo Fabekovec
Maja Franić
Vanja Garaj
Goran Golik
Romano Grozić
Miranda Herceg
Jelenko Herceg
Goran Ivaniš
Ivana Ivanković
Sven Jonke
Željka Jordan
Christoph Katzler
Inja Kavurić
Grajner & Kopilak
Krunoslav Kovač
Damir Kovačević
Dragutin Dado Kovačević
Suzana Kovačević
Goran Kramarić
Ivan Križan
Dino Krpan
Juraj Krstinić
Dejan Kršić
Boris Ljubičić
Igor Ljubičić
Vladimir Madunić
Boris Malešević
Igor Masnjak
Đeki Milatić
Andrea Milovanović
Ira Payer Baletić
Petar Pavić
Zoran Pavlović
Mario Petrak
Danijel Popović
Nikola Radeljković
Ante Rasić
Dejan Dragosavac Rutta
Željko Serdarević
Maša Sirovica
Milan Sivački
Jadranka Soviček
Vladimir Szigeti
Nedjeljko Špoljar
Davor Tomičić
Toni Uroda
Tomo Vlainić
Dubravka Zglavnik
Ana Žaja
Jana Žiljak
Nikola Žinić

(This page)
Design Firm: Studio International
Creative Director, Art Director,
Designer: Boris Ljubicic
Illustrator: Igor Masyar, Igor Ljubicic
Client: Croatian Designers Society

(This page)
Design Firm: RBMM
Creative Director: Robin Ayres
Art Director: Jackson Wang

(Opposite page)
Design Firm: Oh Boy A
Design Company
Creative Director, Art Director:
David Salanitro

Victoria Pohlman
Photographer: Mimi O Chun,
Hunter Wimmer
Client: Artists in Print

(This page)
Creative Director, Art Director,
Designer: Hon Bing Wah
Photographer: Hon Bing Wah
Client: Graphic Arts Association

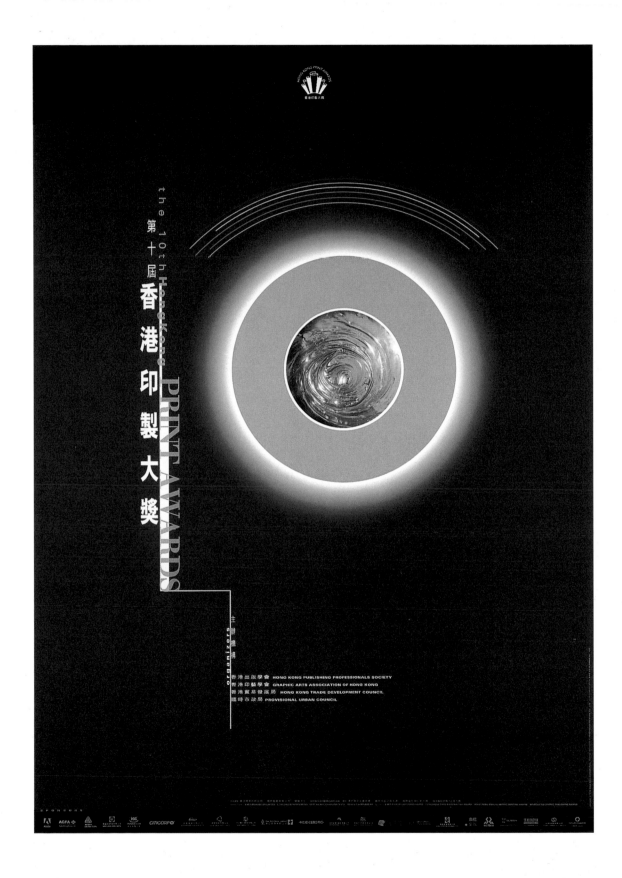

(Opposite page)
Designer: Michael Schwab
Client: Mervyns California

(This spread)
Design Firm: Yeh Design Co Ltd
Creative Director, Art Director,
Designer: Gary Yeh Kuo Sung
Writer: Gary Yeh Kuo Sung

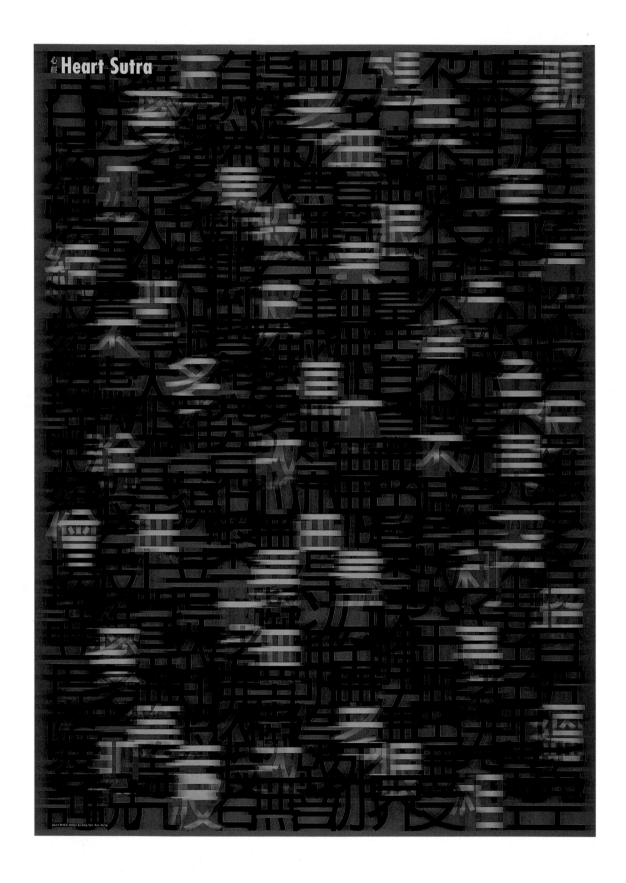

心經 Heart Sutra

(This spread)
Design Firm: Imboden Melchior
Creative Director, Art Director,
Designer: Imboden Melchior
Client: Galerie Chtaslager Stans

INNERSCHWEIZER KÜNSTLER 1998

KUNSTMARKT

SCHMIEDGASSE STANS DI 8. DEZ. 14 - 18 UHR

Jazz Strings

Willisau

Sa 31. Januar 98

20.30 Mohren

Philip Catherine g

Michal Urbaniak viol

Aladar Pege b

(This page)
Design Firm: Viva Dolan
Communcations
Art Director, Designer: Frank Viva
Photographer: Ron Baxter Smith
Client: The Advertising &
Design Club of Canada

(Opposite page)
Design Firm: Niklaus Troxler Design
Creative Director, Art Director,
Designer: Niklaus Troxler
Illustrator: Niklaus Troxler
Client: Jazz in Willisau

(This page)
Design Firm: Emery Vincent Design
Photographer: Earl Carter
Client: Workshop 3000

IDÉE GALLERY TOKYO 99

(This page)
Design Firm: Niklaus Troxler Design
Creative Director, Art Director,
Designer: Niklaus Troxler
Illustrator: Niklaus Troxler
Client: Bosch Silkscreen Company

Ein farbiges Jahr bei Bösch Siebdruck AG Stans/Luzern

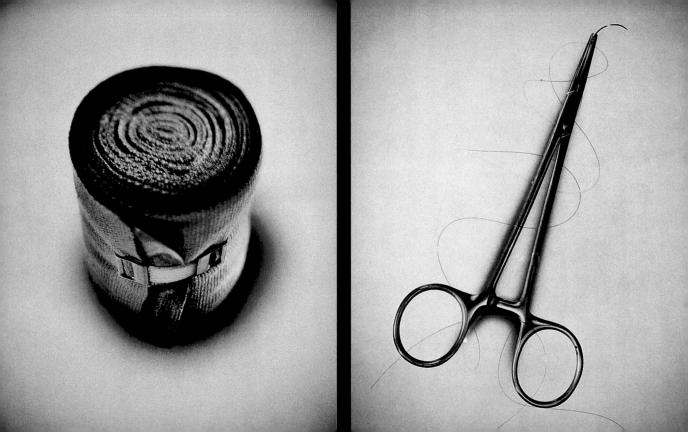

MUSTAFA

10 EKİM – 20 KASIM 1998

HORASAN
ALACA

TEŞVİKİYE SANAT GALERİSİ

KARANLIK

ABDİ İPEKÇİ CADDESİ 18/3 TEŞVİKİYE İSTANBUL TEL: (0212) 241 04 58 - 247 74 75

SERGİ

(This page)
Designer: James Saisakorn
Client: Lincoln Center Fort Collins

(Opposite page)
Design Firm: Savas Cekic Tasarim Ltd
Creative Director, Art Director,
Designer: Savas Cekic
Illustrator: Mustafa Horasan
Client: Mustafa Horasan

The David and Alfred Smart Museum of Art
The University of Chicago
[address text]

[address text]

TRANSIENCE

Chinese Experimental Art at the End of the Twentieth Century

February 18 – April 18, 1999

The David and Alfred Smart
Museum of Art
The University of Chicago

RELATED EVENTS

Except as noted, all events and receptions are free to the public.

Seminar: Chinese Experimental Art at the End of the Twentieth Century
Friday, February 19, 1:30 to 5:00 pm
Cochrane-Woods Art Center, Room 157
3540 South Greenwood Avenue

Featuring artists Cai Guo-Qiang, Hong Hao, Huang Yan, Xu Bing, Zhang Huan, Zhang Peili and Zhang Xiaogang. This event is organized by the Smart Museum and the Consortium Institute for the Humanities, The University of Chicago.

Film Screening: Good Morning, Beijing, directed by Zhang Nuanxin
Saturday, February 20, 2:00 pm
DOC Films, Max Palevsky Cinema, Ida Noyes Hall, 1212 East 59th Street

With an introduction by Tony Rayns, Associate Professor of East Asian Languages and Civilizations, The University of Chicago.

Concert: Min Xiao-Fen
Sunday, March 28, 3:00 pm
Chicago Cultural Center, Preston Bradley Hall, 78 East Washington Avenue

Free event co-sponsored by the Chicago Department of Cultural Affairs as part of the World Music Festival Music Without Borders at the Chicago Cultural Center.

An internationally renowned master of the pipa, Min Xiao-Fen won acclaim with the National Chinese Music Orchestra. She has collaborated with musicians and composers such as Chen Yi, Zhou Long, Bun Ching Lam, Bun Ching Lam, Tan Dun, John Zorn and Derek Bailey. She will perform traditional and contemporary and works on the pipa, a traditional Chinese lute.

Smart Museum Collectors Series
Saturday, March 13, 10:30 to 12:00 am

Exhibition curator Wu Hung and guest lecturer Gao Minglu will lead a gallery tour and discussion for members and will lead a tour. Opportunity for new members of the Smart Museum. Free for Collectors Level members and above. $50 for non-member members. Please call 773.702.0200 for responsibilities and information about becoming a member.

Symposium: Global Perspectives on Contemporary Chinese Art
Saturday, April 17, 9 am to 5 pm
Tarawsky Biological Sciences Learning Center, 924 East 57th Street

Featuring an international group of scholars, curators, and artists, including participants such as Xu Bing, Gao Minglu, Hou Hanru, and others in a conversation moderated by exhibition curator Wu Hung and guest curator Gao Minglu. This symposium is part of a larger conference on the subject of culture, region, nation and the international museum, supported in part by the Freeman Foundation. Other supporters include the Ford and Henry Luce Foundations. Co-sponsored by the Center for East Asian Studies, The University of Chicago. Please call 773.834.2522 for more information or see below.

Public Exhibition Tours
Tuesdays, February 23, March 23 & March 30, April 13, 1:30 pm
Meet in Smart Museum lobby.

Led by University of Chicago advanced docents.

Please call the Smart Museum at 773.702.0572 for more information about these programs.

Opening Reception
Thursday, February 18, 1999
5:30 to 7:30 pm

Please stop by to see this long-awaited exhibition and to join us for the reception. Meetings of our Sunday Breakfast at Chinese Art devotees. The University of Chicago, and co-host the reception for Prof. Wu Hung curator of this exhibition.

The David and Alfred Smart Museum of Art
The University of Chicago

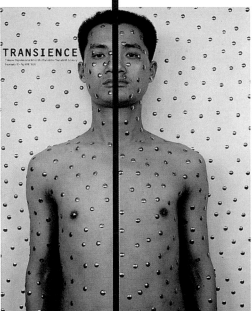

International Logo Festival 98　　Beijing

Sept. 13 - 16　1998　　Beijing Exhibition Center

The Capital Corporation Image Institution (CCII)

International Trademark Exhibition　　International Trademark Festival Design Award　　Seminar of "Corporation Image and Brand Image in the 21st Century"

主办: 首都企业形象研究会　　协办: 国际商标中心　　北京京华广告公司　　鸣谢: 北京国际艺苑皇冠假日饭店

MUSA PAPER LAND
eco

ムーサペーパーランド ［エコ］
古紙配合 100％しかもファンシーな 30 色の "OK エコジャパン"、
豊かな風合いと印刷適性をもちしかもエコロジーをプラスしたファ
ンシーペーパー "OK エコプラス"。ポスター・パッケージ・エ
ディトリアルに紙の表情が生きています。245 名のデザイナー・
イラストレーターが自由にデザインしたタッグシールも OK エ
コプラス、ぜひご覧ください。

6月2日(水) 3日(木) 4日(金) 10:00AM ～ 7:00PM
TBホール 大阪市中央区東心斎橋 2-1-1 TEL：06-6213-3192

主催：ムーサ株式会社 後援：王子製紙株式会社 日本紙パルプ商事株式会社

(This page)
Design Firm: Packaging Create Inc
Art Director: Akio Okumura
Designer: Aki Inoue
Client: Musa

(This page)
Creative Director, Art Director,
Designer: Tadanori Yokoo
Client: Laforet Harajuku Museum

(This page)
Design Firm: Packaging Create Inc
Art Director: Akio Okumura
Designer: Keiko Higashi

Client: Inter Medium Institute
Graduate School

(This page)
Art Director, Designer: Toyotsugu Itoh
Writer: Toyotsugu Itoh
Illustrator: Toyotsugu Itoh
Photographer: Isao Takahashi
Client: Chubu Creators Club

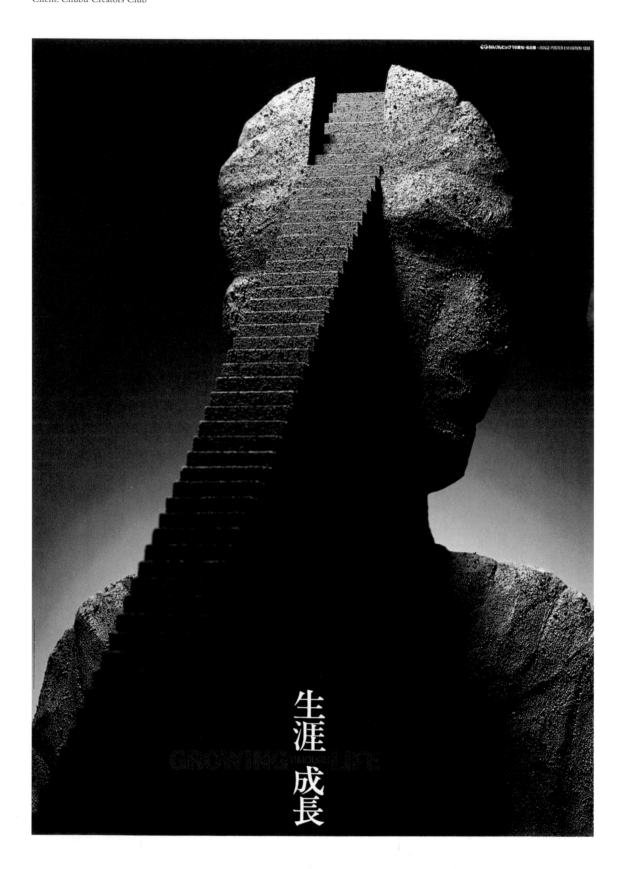

(Opposite page)
Design Firm: Savas Cekic Tasarim Ltd
Creative Direcor, Art Director,
Designer: Savas Cekic
Illustrator: Savas Cekic
Client: Yurt & Dunya

Ferruh BAŞAĞA
Turgut ATALAY
Hasan KAVRUK
Avni ARBAŞ
Hüseyin GEZER
İbrahim BALABAN
Leyla GAMSIZ
Hüseyin BİLİŞİK
Neşet GÜNAL
Mehmet PESEN
Lütfü GÜNAY
Adnan TURANİ
Nuri ABAÇ
Nevzat AKORAL
Şadan BEZEYİŞ
Mustafa ASLIER
Turan EROL
Abdurrahman ÖZTOPRAK
Burhan DOĞANÇAY
Müryide İÇMELİ
Özdemir ALTAN
Dinçer ERİMEZ
Hamiye ÇOLAKOĞLU
Ateş
Salim BUGAY
İlgi ADALAN
Tülay Tura DÖRTTELNE
Hamiz AYDIN
Devrim ERBİL
Dinçer BAŞAHİR
Mustafa AYAZ
Tamer BAŞOĞLU
Mehmet AKSOY
Oktay ANILANMERT
Erdinç BAKLA
Ali CANDAŞ
Mustafa PİLEVNELİ
Süleyman Saim TEKCAN
Güngör GÜNER
Asım İŞLER
Gençer TANER
Nevhiz TANYELİ
Hasan AKIN
Alaaddin AKSOY
Beril ANILANMERT
Ari İsmail TÜREREN
Utku VARLIK
Gökhan ANLAĞAN
Cihat ARAL
Meriç HIZAL
Ergin İNAN
Ferit ÖZŞEN
Atilla ATAR
Noray ARIŞ
İhsan ÇAKICI
Bilal ERDOĞAN
Adem GENÇ
Mehmet GÜLER
Zehra ARAL
Mustafa ATA
Hayati MISIRAN
Mehmet ÖZER
Umur TÜRKER
Muzaffer AKYOL
Mustafa ALTINTAŞ
Zahit BÜYÜKİŞLEYEN
Hasamettin KOÇAN
Balkan Naci İSLİMYELİ
Fevzi KARAKOÇ
Remzi SAVAŞ
Hanefi YETER
Veysel GÜNAY
Ekrem KAHRAMAN
Zeki ARSLAN
Lütfü CULCUL
Cuma ÖCAKLI
Zekai ORMANCI
Sabatay ÖZEN
Sarı TURAN
Tülma TİLİN
Rafet ENIZ
Ahmet MÜDERRİSOĞLU
Yavuz TANYELİ
Hale ARPACIOĞLU
Bubi
Mahmut CELAYIR
Ender GÜZEY
Hasim KONYAR
Benyamin ÖZGÜLTEKİN
Habib AYDOĞDU
İbrahim ÇİFTÇİOĞLU
Tunç TANIŞIK
Meryem ARICAN
Aydın AYAN
Birin ÖCAL
Fuin ÖĞ
Ertuğrul ATEŞ
Orhan BENLİ
Sema BOYANCI
Kemal ÖNSOY
Yunus TONKUŞ
Ruhmi AKSUNGUR
Argun OKUMUŞOĞLU
Emre ZEYTİNOĞLU
Mevsut AKYILDIZ
Kezban Arca BATIBEKİ
Cengiz SAVAŞ
Sergül YETER
Bedri BAYKAM
Alp Tamer ULUKILIÇ
Tayfun ERDOĞMUŞ
Selahattin KARA
İrfan ÖNÜREN
Ali KOTAN
Timur ÇELİK
Mehmet ÇETİNER
Ercan SAĞLAM
Selahattin YILDIRIM
Mustafa Sahin AKTUĞ
Halim ÇELİKER
Turhan ÇETİN
Tanju DEMİREI
Namiaz DEMİRKALP
Bahar KOCAMAN
Huşnu DOKAK
Dinh HEKİMOĞLU
Atilla İLKYAZ
Devabit KARA
Cebrail ÖTKÜN
Avni ÖZTOPÇU
Kemal TUFAN
Arzu BAŞARAN
Cemit ERGON
A.Onay AKBAŞ
Mustafa PANCAR
Adil SALIH
Şükriz AKSOY
Harun ANTAKYALI
Saim ERKEN
Mustafa HORASAN
Zafer MİNTAŞ
Hakan ONUR
Cezmi ORMAN
Ferhat ÖZGÜR
Ayhan YILMAZ
Murat ÇELİK
Tansel TÜRKDOĞAN
Canan ATALAY
Ayşe Sibel KEDİK
Deniz ORKUŞ
Ayşen URFALIOĞLU
Sevinç AKKAYA
Dilek ÇETİNER
Mutlu BAŞKAYA
Allan ÇELEN
R. Yiğit YAZICI
Nihal KEMANKAŞLI

(This page)
Design Firm: Paul Davis Studio
Creative Direcor: Silas Rhodes
Art Director, Designer: Paul Davis
Illustrator: Paul Davis
Client: School of Visual Arts

(Opposite page)
Design Firm: Sommese Design
Creative Direcor, Art Director,
Designer: Lanny Sommese
Illustrator: Lanny Sommese
Client: Central Pennsylvania Festival
of the Arts

(This page, left)
Design Firm: Yu Design Co
Creative Direcor, Art Director,
Designer: Yu Ming Lung
Client: Yu Design Co

(This page, right; Opposite page)
Design Firm: Yu Design Co
Creative Direcor, Art Director,
Designer: Yu Ming Lung
Client: Chinese Poster Design Association

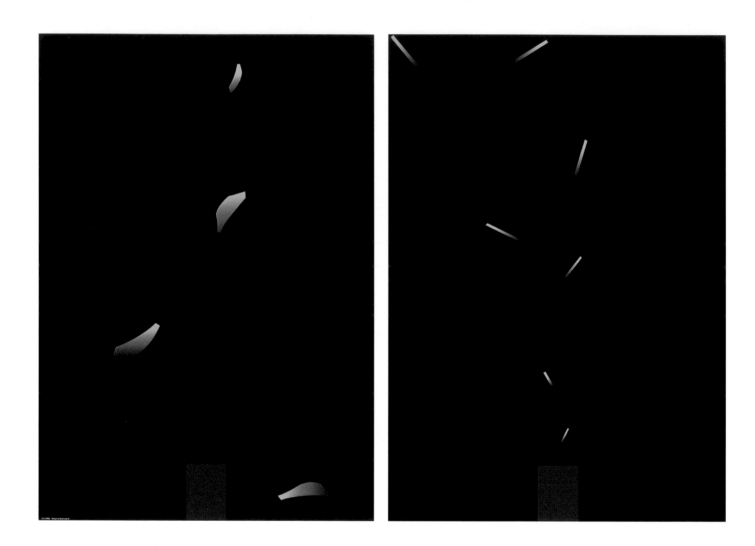

(This page)
Design Firm: Leslie Chan Design Co Ltd
Creative Direcor, Art Director:
Leslie Chan Wing Kei
Designer: Leslie Chan Wing Kei,
Clair Ger
Photographer: Larcher Chao
Client: The Chinese Information
& Culture Center

TAIWAN IMAGE POSTER DESIGN IN NEW YORK

DATE JULY 17 - AUGUST 28,1998. TIME 10:00 A.M.-5:00 P.M.
VENUE TAIPEI GALLERY NEW YORK,NEW YORK
ORGANIZER:THE DESIGN ASSOCIATION OF THE REPUBLIC OF CHINA
CO-ORGANIZERS:THE CHINESE INFORMATION AND CULTURE CENTER OF
THE TAIPEI ECONOMIC & CULTURAL OFFICE IN NEW YORK / CHINESE POSTER DESIGN ASSOCIATION

(This page)
Design Firm: Leslie Chan Design Co Ltd   Clair Ger
Creative Direcor, Art Director: Photographer: Justin Chiv
Leslie Chan Wing Kei   Client: Auspic Paper Co Ltd
Designer: Leslie Chan Wing Kei,

(Opposite page)
Design Firm: Leslie Chan Design Co Ltd   Photographer: Stephen Ip
Creative Direcor, Art Director,   Client: The Council for
Designer: Leslie Chan Wing Kei   Cultural Affairs Republic

DESiGN de TAiWAN... d'art, Affiches

de 15 septembre au 23

du octobre

vendredi

de 10h à

de 12h30

à 17h30 et de 13h30 de

* ORGANISATEURS! Association de Design de TAiWAN

d'Affiches et d'information

à Paris

Centre Culturel de TAiwan

avec le soutien du Conseil Culturel

Reihnades Affaires Culturelllg*

(This page)
Design Firm: Kan & Lau Design
Consultants
Creative Direcor, Art Director:
Tai Keung Kan
Designer: Tai Keung Kan,

Wai Hung Lam
Photographer: CK Wong
Client: China National Academy of
Fine Arts

Kan

Tai-

Keung

Design

Show

靳

埭

強

設

展

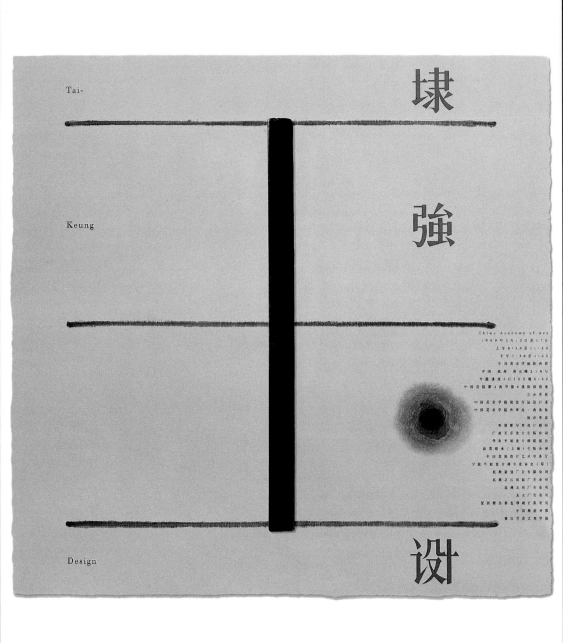

INTERACTION

SHANGHAI INTERNATIONAL POSTER INVITATION EXHIBITION '99

(This page)
Design Firm: Kan & Lau
Design Consultants
Art Director, Designer:
Freeman Lau Siu Hong

Illustrator: Ray Ho
Client: Shanghai Graphic
Designers Association

Art Director, Designer:
Freeman Lau Siu Hong
Client: Kan & Lau Design Consultants

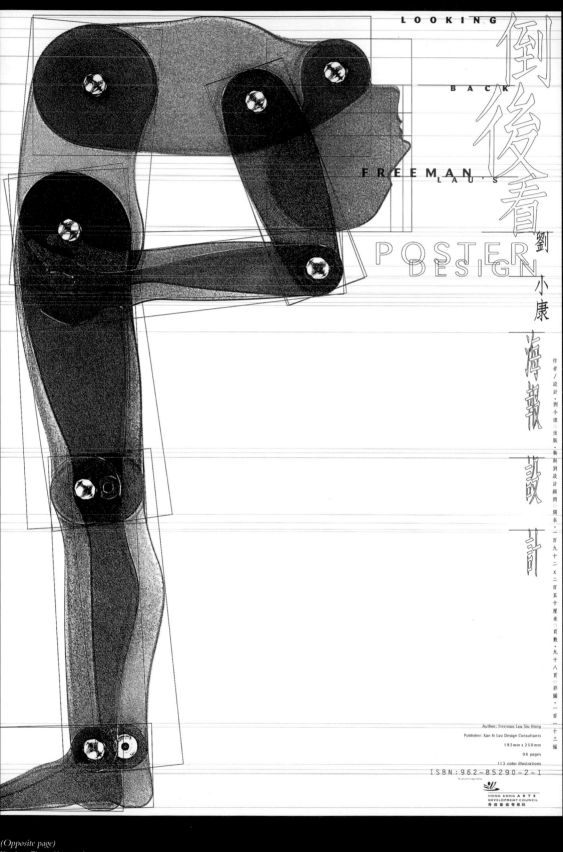

LOOKING

BACK

FREEMAN'S
LAU'S

POSTER
DESIGN

倒後看

劉小康

海報

設計

作者／設計・劉小康○出版・靳與劉設計顧問○開本・一百九十二 X 二百五十厘米○頁數・九十八頁○彩圖・一百二十三幅

Author: Freeman Lau Siu Hong
Publisher: Kan & Lau Design Consultants
192 mm x 250 mm
96 pages
113 color illustrations
ISBN: 962-85290-2-1

HONG KONG ARTS
DEVELOPMENT COUNCIL
香港藝術發展局

(Opposite page)
Design Firm: Kan & Lau
Design Consultants
Creative Director, Art Director,
Designer: Tai Keung Kan
Client: Shanghai Graphic Designers

INTERACTION

SHISEIDO

SHISEIDO

vocalise

say. ask. promise. cry. whisper. scream. vocalise.

(This spread; Next page)
Design Firm: Shiseido Co Ltd
Creative Director, Art Director:
Naomi Yamamoto

Designer: Saiko Kawahara
Photographer: Kaz Kiriya
Client: Shiseido

(Opposite page)
Design Firm: Dennis Ascienzo
Creative Director, Art Director:
Nedjeljko Matura
Designer: Dennis Ascienzo
Photographer: Nedjeljko Matura

(This page)
Design Firm: Planet Design Company
Creative Director, Art Director:
Dana Lytle
Designer: Dan Ibarra

Writer: John Besmer, Seth Bardon
Illustrator: Dan Ibarra
Client: Rollerblade; RB Shoes

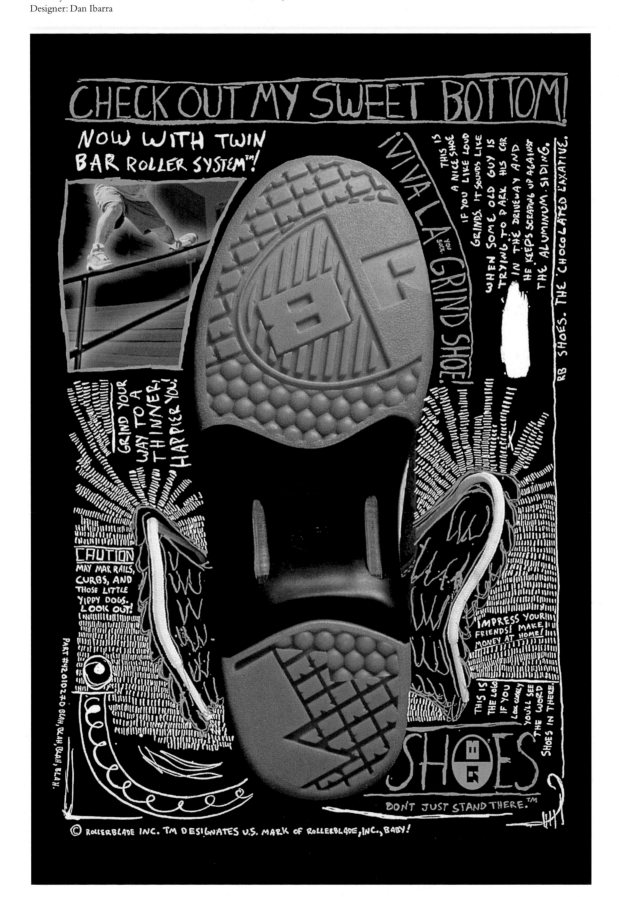

(This page)
Creative Director, Art Director:
Kum Jun Park
Designer: Jong In Jung, Jong Pil Lee
Writer: Joon Young Bae

Illustrator: Han Kim
Client: Visual Information Design
Association of Korea

(Opposite page)
Design Firm: Lure
Designer: Paul Mastriani, Jeff Matz
Client: Orlando UCF
Shakespeare Festival

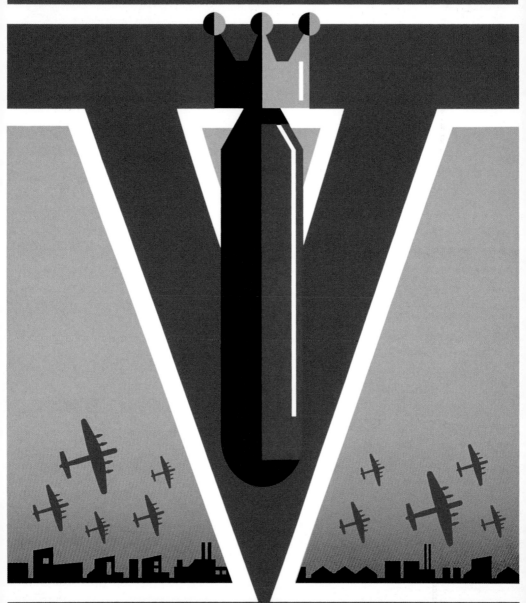

CELEBRATING OUR TENTH ANNIVERSARY SEASON 1989-1999
THE ORLANDO-UCF SHAKESPEARE FESTIVAL PRESENTS

HENRY V

APRIL 7 THROUGH MAY 7
WALT DISNEY AMPHITHEATER | LAKE EOLA PARK
TICKETS $6 TO $35 | BOX OFFICE 407 245 0985 EXT 1

IN REPERTORY WITH TWELFTH NIGHT SPONSORED BY NATIONSBANK

DESIGN LORE

(This page)
Design Firm: Lanny Sommese
Creative Director, Art Director,
Designer: Lanny Sommese
Illustrator: Lanny Sommese
Client: Central Penn Festival of the Arts

(Opposite page)
Design Firm: TBWA GGT
Simons Palmer
Creative Director: Trevor Beattie
Art Director: Paul Belford
Designer: Paul Belford, Alan Kitching
Writer: Nigel Roberts
Client: Kew Gardens

KEWGARDENSKEWGARDENSKEW

3000 INCREDIBLE BULBS. LIKE PICCADILLY CIRCUS BUT SMELLS NICER.

1-30 APRIL THE HIPPEASTRUM CELEBRATION

INDEPENDENT FILM
IT HAS A MIND
OF ITS OWN

23RD ANNUAL ATLANTA FILM & VIDEO FESTIVAL JUNE 12-20

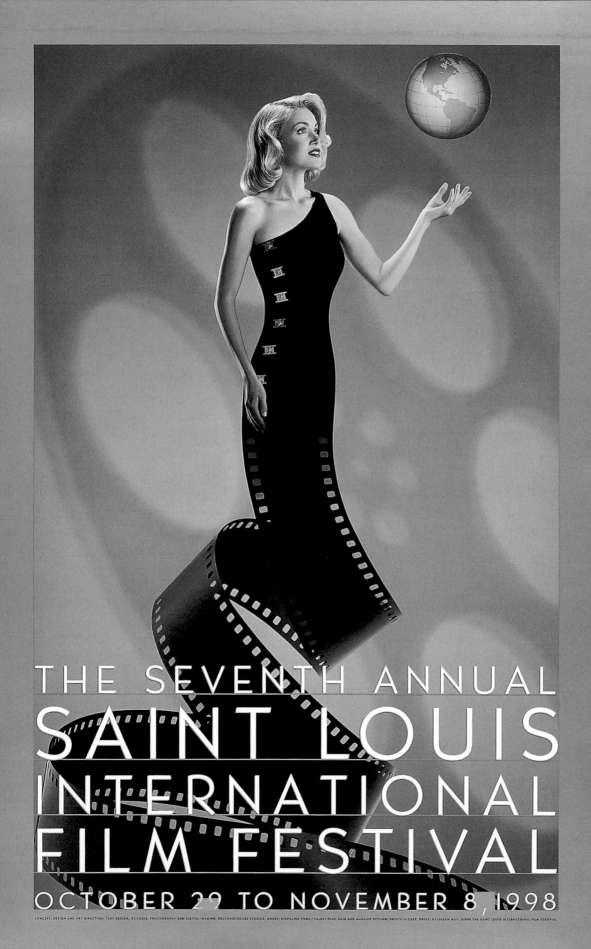

THE SEVENTH ANNUAL
SAINT LOUIS
INTERNATIONAL
FILM FESTIVAL
OCTOBER 29 TO NOVEMBER 8, 1998

Can kick the crap out of mints twice its size.

Blitz. The tiny power mint with a profit per square inch that has the big guys running scared. See us at
NCA Show booth #2418, call us at 1.888.254.8948 or check out www.blitzpowermints.com

Gutes Essen statt böser Krieg: Das Restaurant in der ehemaligen Stettenkaserne.

MORE THAN FOOD

Gutes Essen statt böser Krieg: Das Restaurant in der ehemaligen Stettenkaserne.

MORE THAN FOOD

Menü

Gutes Essen statt böser Krieg: Das Restaurant in der ehemaligen Stettenkaserne.

MORE THAN FOOD

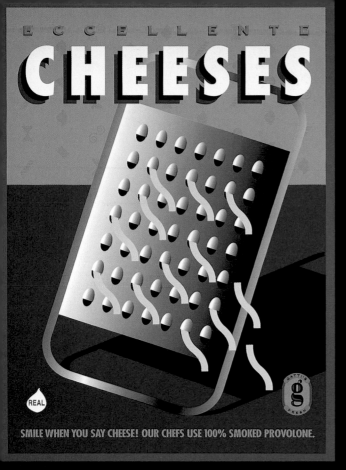

ECCELLENTE

CHEESES

REAL

SMILE WHEN YOU SAY CHEESE! OUR CHEFS USE 100% SMOKED PROVOLONE.

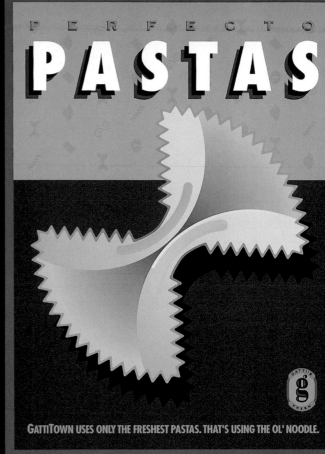

PERFECTO

PASTAS

GATTITOWN USES ONLY THE FRESHEST PASTAS. THAT'S USING THE OL' NOODLE.

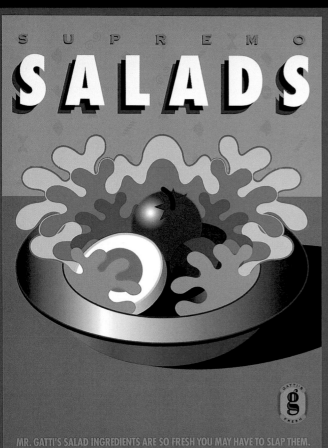

SUPREMO

SALADS

MR. GATTI'S SALAD INGREDIENTS ARE SO FRESH YOU MAY HAVE TO SLAP THEM.

SAPOROSO

SAUCES

Heinz

SHHHHHHHH! PREPARED TO PERFECTION WITH 12 SECRET HERBS AND SPICES.

Pure TEA. Pure JUICE. Pure BLISS.™

(Opposite page)
Design Firm: Denner Merlicek
& Bergmann
Creative Director: Mariusz Jan Denner
Art Director: Hubert Goldnagl
Writer: Jan Froscher

(This page)
Design Firm: KG Olsson
Art Director, Designer: KG Olsson
Client: Skissernas Museum Lund

SKULPTUR
INFÖR ÅR TVÅTUSEN
SKISSERNAS MUSEUM
FINNGATAN 2 LUND
13 JUNI - 26 SEPT 1999

(Opposite page)
Creative Director, Art Director,
Designer: Tadanori Yokoo
Photographer: Norihiro Veno
Client: Xaravel

(This page)
Design Firm: Grafik Communications
Creative Director: Judy Kirpich
Art Director, Designer: Johnny
Vitorovich
Client: National Museum of the
American Indian

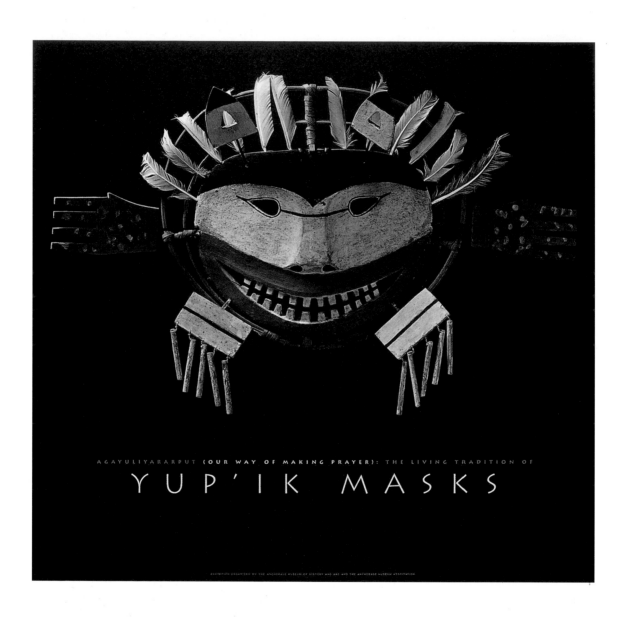

AGAYULIYARARPUT **(OUR WAY OF MAKING PRAYER)**: THE LIVING TRADITION OF

YUP'IK MASKS

EXHIBITION ORGANIZED BY THE ANCHORAGE MUSEUM OF HISTORY AND ART AND THE ANCHORAGE MUSEUM ASSOCIATION

(Opposite page)
Design Firm: Momentum Design
Creative Director: Sandy Lee, Tom Hunt
Designer: Sandy Lee
Client: Asian Art Museum

HARU MATSURI AT THE ASIAN

THE ART OF IKEBANA

An exhibition of floral arrangements

from five Ikebana Schools

OPENING NIGHT GALA

TUESDAY, APRIL 6TH, 1999   6:30PM

$100 per person

Event Chair Rosemary Yagi Townsend

For more information call 415-557-6988

EXHIBITION AND LECTURE SERIES

WEDNESDAY, APRIL 7TH - SUNDAY, APRIL 11TH

Asian Art Museum of San Francisco

Golden Gate Park

This goblet may very well hold spirits.

MINT MUSEUM OF CRAFT + DESIGN

Look closely and you can see an entire culture in this basket.

MINT MUSEUM OF CRAFT + DESIGN

(This page)
Design Firm: Paul Davis Studio
Creative Director, Art Director,
Designer: Paul Davis
Illustrator: Paul Davis
Client: Music Festival of the Hamptons

(Opposite page)
Art Director: Brooks Branch
Designer: Michael Schwab
Illustrator: Michael Schwab
Client: Bruce McGaw Galleries

(This spread)
Design Firm: GSD&M
Art Director: Matt Davis
Writer: Kent Portman

Photographer: Andre Yates
Client: Metropolitan Winds

A TRIBUTE TO THE MUSIC OF
JOHN WILLIAMS

ORIGINAL MUSIC FROM
JAWS

STAR WARS • E.T. • JURASSIC PARK • SUPERMAN • RAIDERS OF THE LOST ARK

BASS PERFORMANCE HALL
JULY 4, 1999 · FT. WORTH
STAR TICKETS (888) 597-7827 &
ALBERTSON'S GROCERY STORES

METROPOLITAN
Winds
RANDOL BASS
MUSIC DIRECTOR AND CONDUCTOR

MEYERSON SYMPHONY CENTER
JULY 11, 1999 · DALLAS
DILLARD'S (800) 654-9545 &
DILLARD'S DEPARTMENT STORES

(Next spread)
Design Firm: The Martin Agency
Creative Director: John Mahoney
Art Director: Jayanta Jenkins

Writer: Scott Strippling
Client: The Richmond Symphony

★ RICHMOND ★
SYMPHONY
P R E S E N T S
IN CONCERT
the best show
IN '98 FEATURING
SCHUBERT
WITH SPECIAL GUEST
DVORAK
JAN. 18 TREDEGAR
SUN. 5PM IRON WORKS
ALL AGES SHOW $10 ★ CALL 788-1212 ★ FREE PIZZA ★ COLD BEER BRING YOUR EARS

SPONSORED BY:
ALAN NEWMAN
RESEARCH

HATCH SHOW PRINT · NASHVILLE, TENN.

THE RICHMOND SYMPHONY PRESENTS
A NIGHT OF LEGENDS
FEATURING
LUDWIG VAN BEETHOVEN
WITH
MOZART AND ALSO RAVEL!

SUN MAY 3 - 5 Pm
TREDEGAR IRON WORKS

★ ALL AGES SHOW ★
FREE PIZZA! COLD BEER - ADV TIX $10
CALL 788-1212

SPREAD THE WORD

Monday

NOVEMBER 23 1998

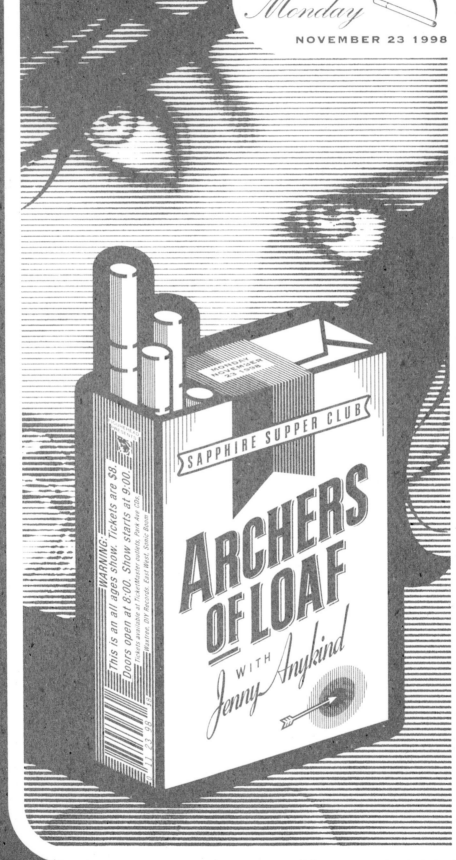

SAPPHIRE SUPPER CLUB

ARCHERS OF LOAF

WITH *Jenny Anykind*

WARNING: This is an all ages show. Tickets are $8. Doors open at 8:00. Show starts at 9:00. Tickets available at TicketMaster outlets, Park Ave CDs, Waxtree, DIY Records, East West, Sonic Boom

FIGUREHEAD AND PARK AVE CDS PRESENT

SAPPHIRE SUPPER CLUB

Elliott Smith

with no.2

TEN DOLLARS GENERAL ADMISSION

DOORS OPEN AT 8:00 SHOW AT 9:00

THIS IS AN ALL AGES SHOW

TICKETS AT ALL TICKETMASTER LOCATIONS

PARK AVE CDS, WAX TREE, SONIC BOOM

AND EAST WEST RECORDS

MONDAY
March 15

1999.5.29

AKI TAKAHASHI PIANO CONCERT AT SPRING HALL, KASUGA CITY

(Previous spread)
Design Firm: Lure
Designer: Jeff Matz
Illustrator: Jeff Matz
Client: Figurehead

(Opposite page)
Design Firm: Osimi Design Co
Art Director, Designer: Tamotsu Oshimi
Photographer: Yukino Nakanishi
Client: Kasuga City Spring Hall

(This page)
Design Firm: Williamsburg Art Works
Creative Director, Art Director,
Designer: Keith Campbell
Client: Girls Against Boys

THE CONNECTICUT GRAND OPERA & ORCHESTRA PRESENTS DONIZETTI'S

LUCIA DI LAMMERMOOR

LAURENCE GILGORE, GENERAL DIRECTOR

Saturday, May 1, 1999, 8pm

The Palace Theatre, Stamford

For Tickets: 203-325-4466

Saturday, May 8, 1999, 8pm

Klein Memorial Auditorium, Bridgeport

For Tickets: 203-359-0009

Sung in Italian with USTitles

(This spread)
Designer: Agnes Rozmann
Photographer: Agnes Rozmann
Client: French Institute in Budapest

(Opposite page)
Design Firm: Tom Fowler Inc
Art Director, Designer: Tom Fowler
Illustrator: Tom Fowler
Client: Connecticut Grand Opera
& Orchestra

(This page)
Design Firm: Packaging Create Inc
Art Director: Akio Okumura
Designer: Yasuyo Fukumoto
Client: Oji Paper Co Ltd/Japan Pult &
Paper/Musa

廃食用油を燃料につかう
私達は家庭から排出される廃食用油などが
水を汚染するのを防ぐため、回収しボイラーで
燃焼させて紙をつくるエネルギーの一部として
利用しています。

Use waste cooking oil as fuel
We collect waste cooking oil from houses, and
use them as fuels for manufacturing papers to
avoid their polluting the sea.

(This page)
Design Firm: Packaging Create Inc
Art Director: Akio Okumura
Designer: Yasuyo Fukumoto
Client: Oji Paper Co Ltd/Japan Pult &
Paper/Musa

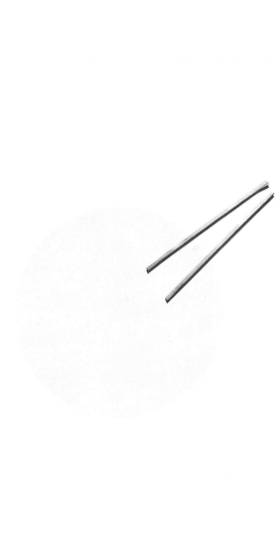

割箸から紙をつくる
私達はゴミ問題や資源の再利用を考え、
使用ずみの割箸を回収し木材チップに混ぜて
紙の素材にしています。古紙箱の割箸で
15箱のティッシュペーパーがつくれます。

Make papers from chopsticks
We think about recycles of garbage and
resources. We make use of disposable
chopsticks by mixing them into wooden chips
for manufacturing papers. We can make 15
boxes of tissue papers from 7500 pairs of
chopsticks.

(This page)
Design Firm: Packaging Create Inc
Art Director: Akio Okumura
Designer: Yasuyo Fukumoto
Client: Oji Paper Co Ltd/Japan
Pult & Paper Co

(Opposite page; top left, top right)
Design Firm: Imageneering
Creative Director: Alpo Raina
Art Director, Designer: Esa Nieminen
Writer: Alpo Raina
Photographer: Lane Kelho
Client: Stora Enso Timber

古紙100%配合 OK エコジャパン
やわらかな手ざわりを持ち、色彩は30色。しかも
古紙100%でつくられた新しいファンシーペーパー。
社会性と美しさを両立させました。

eco

Mixing 100% of used papers. OK Eco Japan.
It has a soft texture, and has 30 colors. It is a new
fancy paper made from 100% of used papers. It
established both socially and aesthetics.

(Opposite page; bottom left, bottom right)
Design Firm: Joao Machado LDA
Creative Director, Art Director,
Designer: Joao Machado

Illustrator: Joao Machado
Client: SDP Sociedade de
Distribuicao de Papel

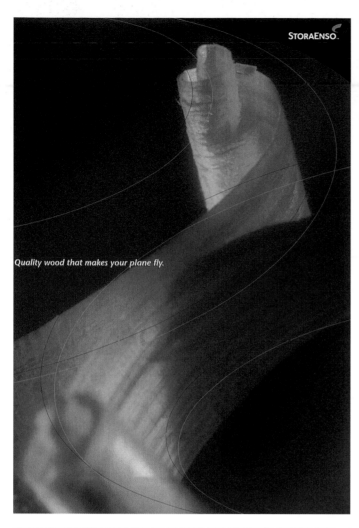

Quality wood that makes your plane fly.

StoraEnso.

A new perspective on timber trade.

StoraEnso.

Papéis Carreira

Papéis Carreira

This is Influence Gloss®.   Number (3) coated freesheet web paper. Beautiful, bright power for any big idea.

Champion Web.

turn up the volume on your ideas.™

(This page)
Design Firm: Imboden Melchior
Creative Director: Imboden Melchior
Photographer: Imboden Melchior
Client: Tunikunz Juwellier Luzern

(This page)
Design Firm: Imboden Melchior
Creative Director: Imboden Melchior
Photographer: Imboden Melchior
Client: Luzern-Stans-Engelberg Railway

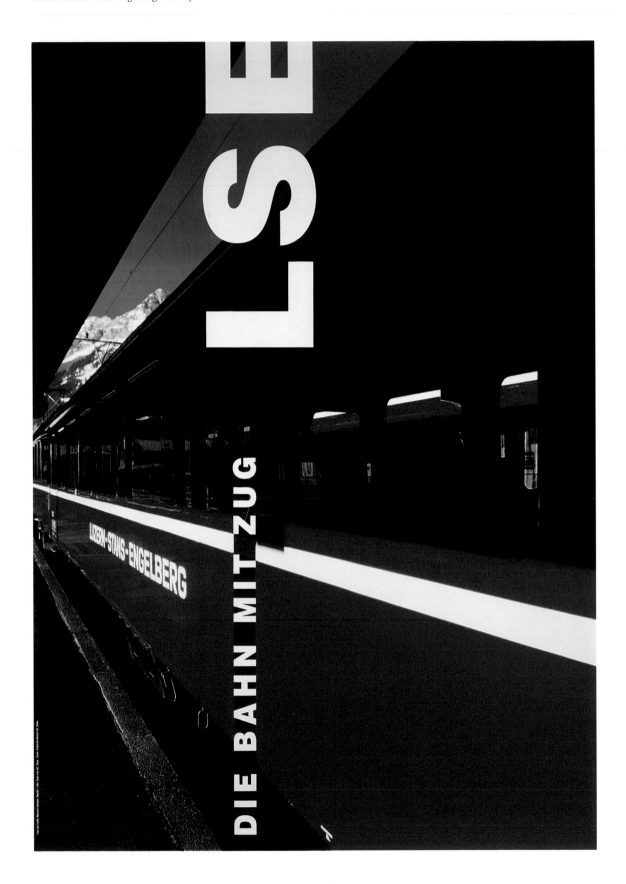

PHIL BEKKER   404 • 688 • 5997

Design Firm: EAI
Creative Director, Art Director,
Designer: Phil Bekker

Photographer: Phil Bekker
Client: Phil Bekker Photography

PHIL BEKKER   404 • 688 • 5997

(This page)
Design Firm: Wang Xu & Associates Ltd
Creative Director, Art Director,
Designer: Wang Xu
Photographer: Liu Wei Xiong
Client: Shenzhen Graphic Designers
Association

(Opposite page)
Design Firm: The Pushpin Group Inc
Illustrator: Seymour Chwast
Client: The Hague Appeal for Peace

PEACE
A HUMAN
RIGHT
HAGUE APPEAL
FOR PEACE
MAY 11-15, 1999
THE HAGUE
OFFICE 777 UN PLAZA
NEW YORK, NY 10017
TEL: 212 687 2623
hap99@igc.apc.org
www.haguepeace.org
or, c/o IALANA, Anna
Paulownastraat 103,
2518 BC The Hague,
THE NETHERLANDS
tel +31 70 363 4484
ialana@antenna.nl

NO GO

Designer: Luba Lukova
Illustrator: Luba Lukova
Client: Luba Lukova

SUDAN

(Opposite page)
Design Firm: William Eisner
& Associates

198

THE

CONSTITUTION GUARANTEES

THAT WE ALWAYS HAVE A

President.

BUT WHEN WAS *THE* LAST TIME WE

— HAD A LEADER? —

☆ ☆ ☆

199

There is a difference between wanting to be President of the United States and wanting to serve the American people in the office of the President. One is the aspiration of a politician, ending with election. The other is the aspiration of someone who sees election as a means to a higher goal of public service.

For Steve Forbes the ultimate goal has always been to serve the American people.

He possesses strong leadership skills from years of executive experience. And his financial independence allows him to champion an agenda designed to serve the public, rather than special interest groups.

By looking outside career politicians and politics as usual, America can experience a new birth of freedom. But we the people have to make it happen.

For more information, or to become a volunteer for the Steve Forbes for America/Steve Forbes for President campaign call 1-800-706-0004. Or visit the National Online Headquarters at www.Forbes2000.com.

— STEVE FORBES *FOR* PRESIDENT —

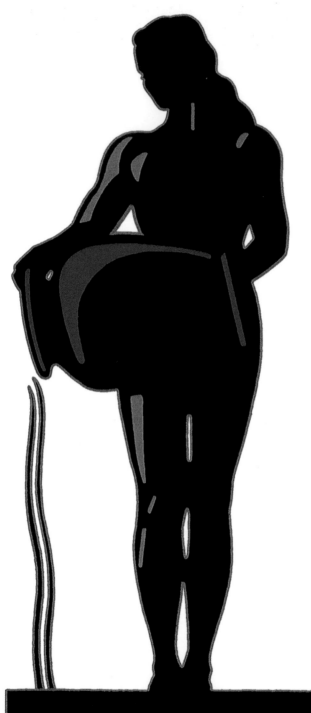

Touch!

(Opposite page)
Designer: Michael Schwab
Illustrator: Michael Schwab
Client: Digital Pond

(This page)
Design Firm: RBMM
Creative Director, Art Director,
Designer, Illustrator: Horacio Cobos
Client: Williamson

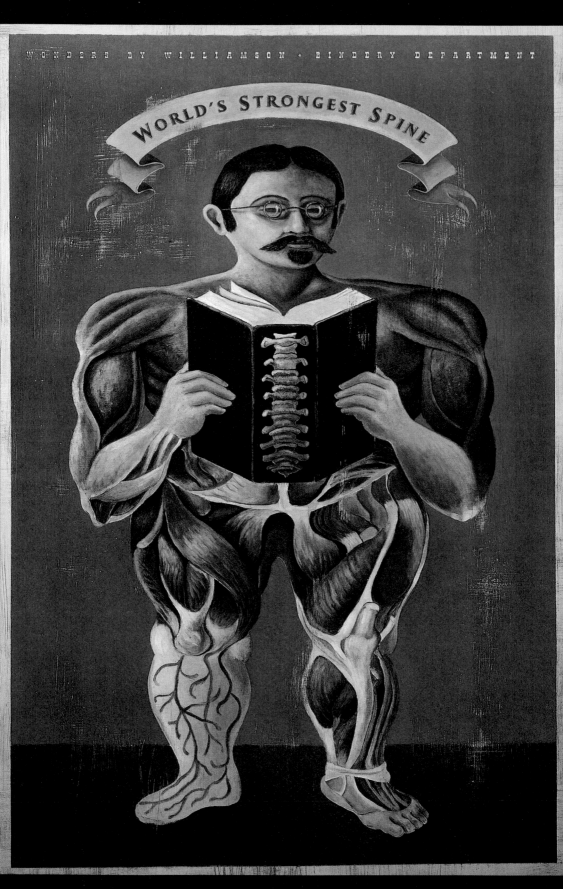

WONDERS BY WILLIAMSON · BINDERY DEPARTMENT

WORLD'S STRONGEST SPINE

(Opposite page)
Design Firm: Oden Marketing   Writer: Bret Terwilleger, Katie Price

lORINTING...

The 10th Hong Kong
Print Awards
Poster Exhibition

PROFESSION *of* PERFECTION

HEIDELBERG

(This page)
Design Firm: BBI Studio Inc
Art Director: Zempaku Suzuki
Designer: Hiroshi Yano, Yohko Fujita
Writer: Nob Ogasawara
Client: BBI Studio Inc

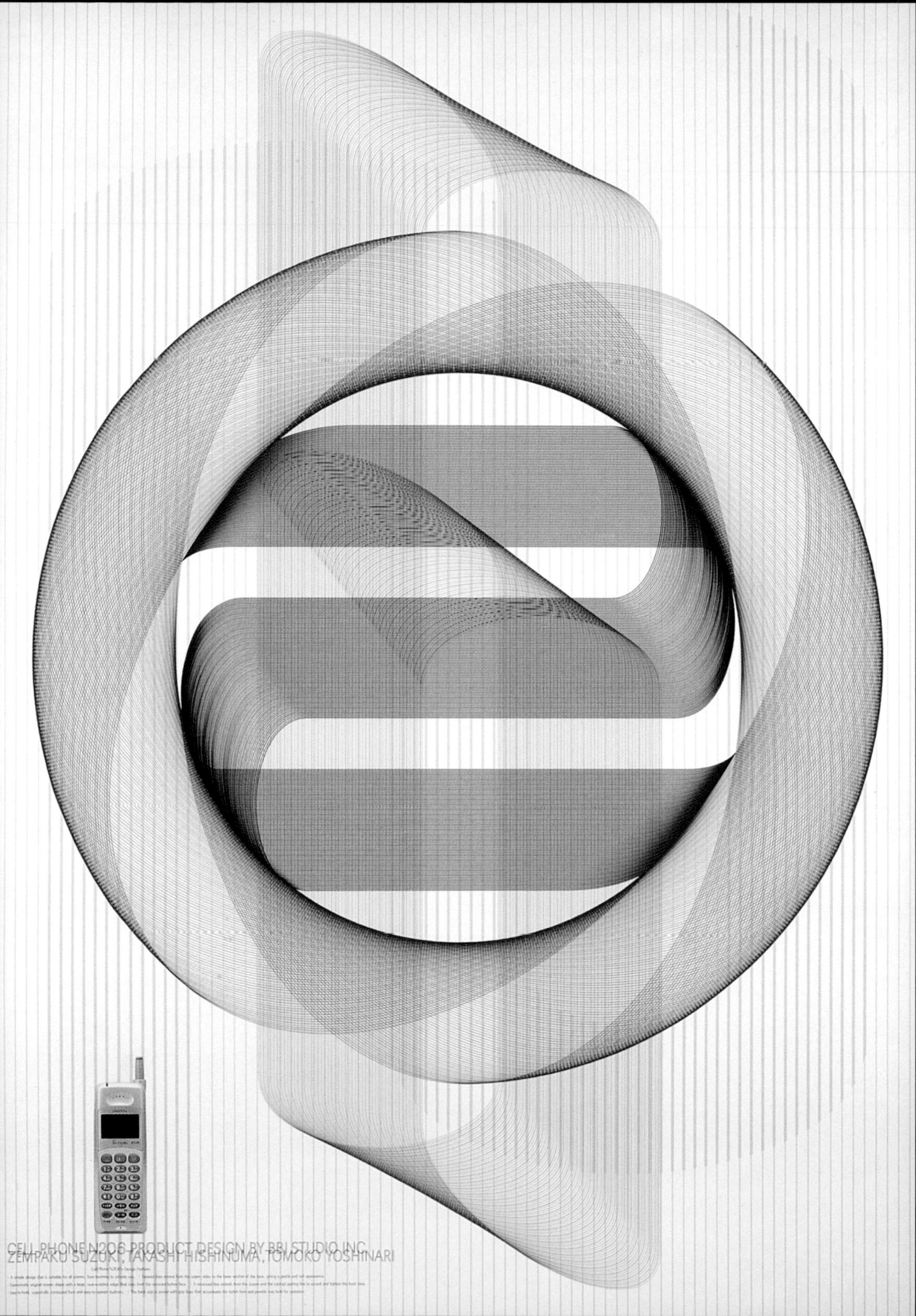

CELL PHONE N206 PRODUCT DESIGN BY BBI STUDIO INC.
ZEMPAKU SUZUKI, TAKASHI HISHINUMA, TOMOKO YOSHINARI

(This page, top)
Design Firm: DDB Needham New York
Creative Director: David Nathanson,
Giff Crosby
Art Director: David Nathanson
Writer: E Schulzinger, Giff Crosby
Client: Lockheed Martin

(This page, bottom)
Design Firm: DDB Needham New York
Creative Director: David Nathanson,
Giff Crosby
Art Director: David Nathanson
Writer: Giff Crosby
Photographer: E Schulzinger
Client: Lockheed Martin

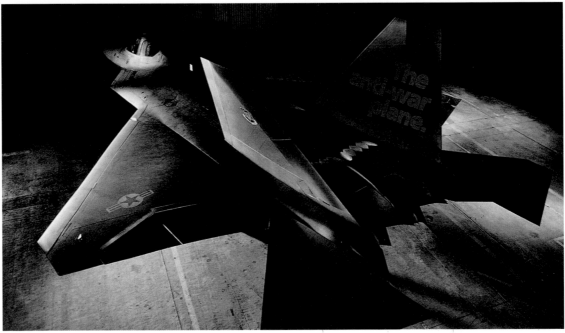

(This page, top)
Design Firm: DDB Needham New York
Creative Director: David Nathanson,
Giff Crosby
Art Director: David Nathanson
Writer: E Schulzinger, Giff Crosby
Client: Lockheed Martin

(This page, bottom)
Design Firm: DDB Needham New York
Creative Director: David Nathanson,
Giff Crosby
Art Director: David Nathanson
Writer: Giff Crosby
Photographer: E Schulzinger
Client: Lockheed Martin

performance skate 1999

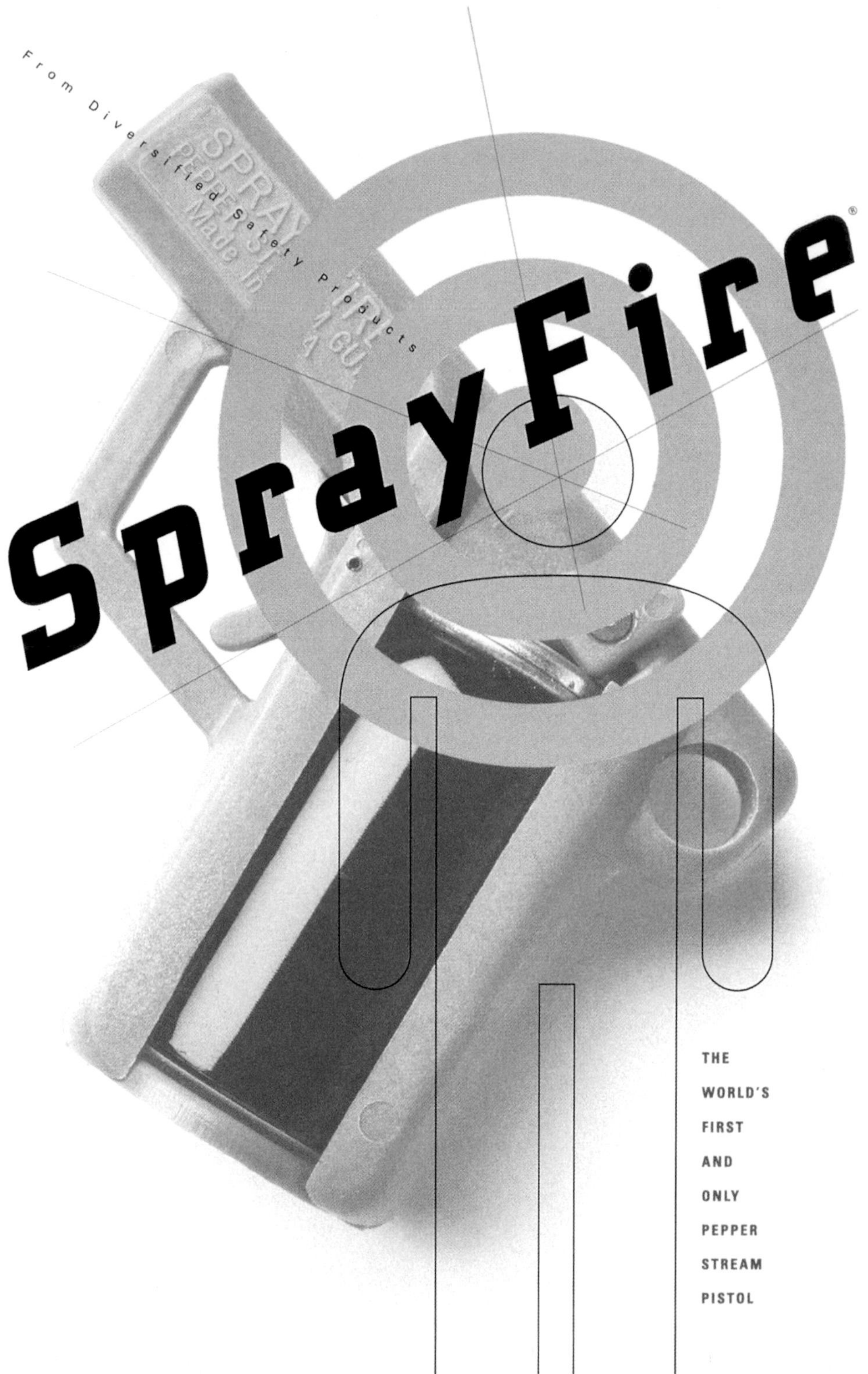

From Diversified Safety Products

SprayFire®

THE
WORLD'S
FIRST
AND
ONLY
PEPPER
STREAM
PISTOL

(This page)
Design Firm: Fitzgerald & Co
Creative Director: Hal Barber
Art Director, Designer: Rob Kottkamp
Writer: Rob Kottkamp
Client: Quikrete
Client: Diversified Products

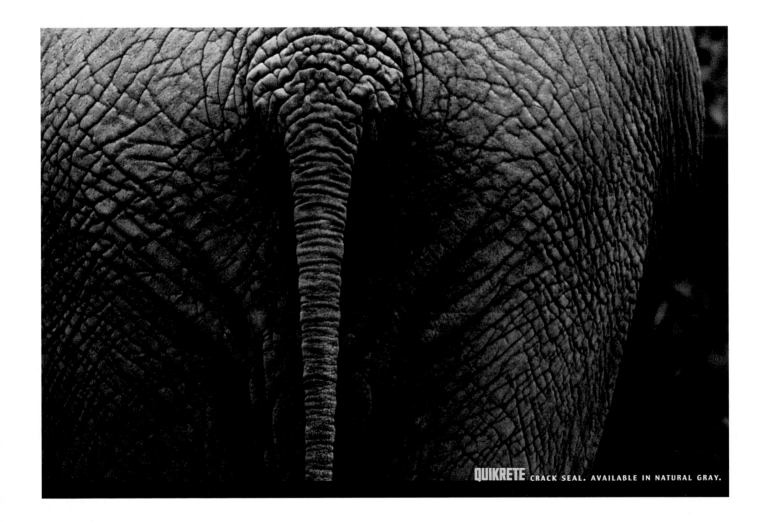

(Opposite page)
Creative Director, Designer: Ted Fabella
Client: Diversified Products

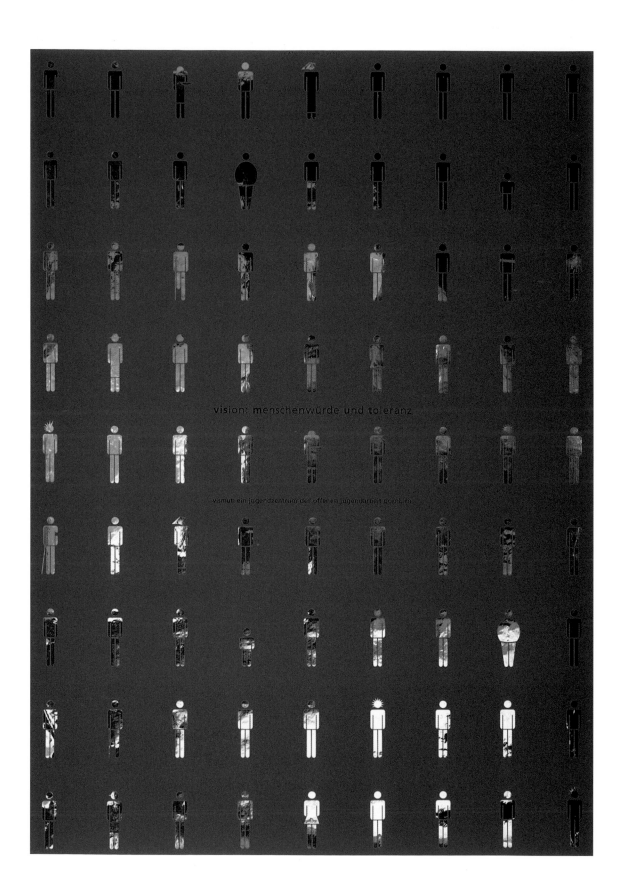

(This page)
Design Firm: Lowe &
Partners/Monsoon
Creative Director: Ng Khee Jin
Art Director: Thomas Yang
Writer: James Lim
Client: Coalition for Nuclear
Disarmament

(Opposite page)
Creative Director: Hans Joachim Goegl
Art Director: Gunter Kassegger
Client: Vismut Jugendhaus

WHITES ONLY

Thanks to Martin Luther King, Jr., signs like this don't exist anymore. Remember him on January 18th.

COLORED

Thanks to Martin Luther King, Jr., signs like this don't exist anymore. Remember him on January 18th.

(This page)
Design Firm: Cyclone
Designer: Traci Daberko, Dennis Clouse
Photographer: Marco Prozzo
Client: Massage Therapists of Seattle

(Opposite page)
Design Firm: Claude Kuhn
Art Director, Designer: Claude Kuhn
Client: Tierpark Dahlholzlibern

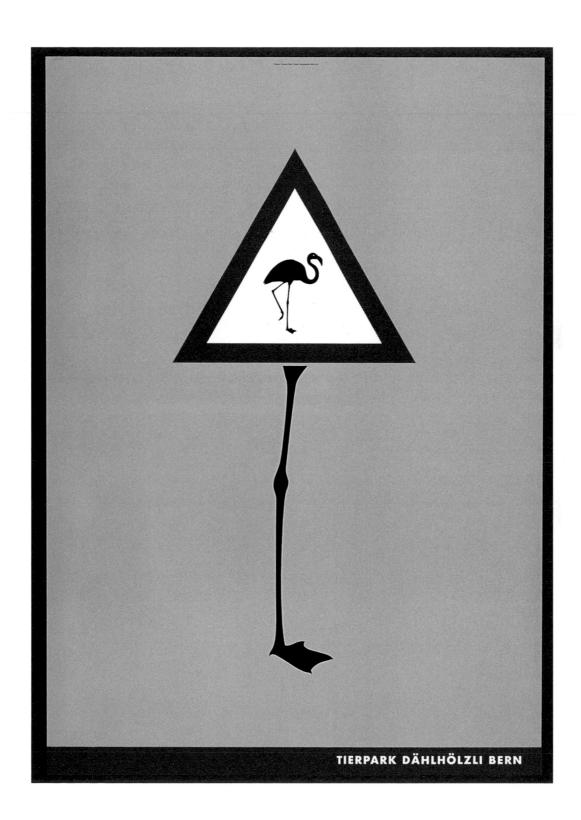

TIERPARK DÄHLHÖLZLI BERN

(This page)
Design Firm: Demner Merlicek & Bergmann
Creative Director: Mariusz Demner, E Sauter, Bernhard Grafl
Writer: Rosa Haider, Andrea Barth
Illustrator: Alexander Krempler
Photographer: Robert Marksteiner
Client: News Verlagsgesmbh & Co KG

(This page)
Design Firm: Oakley Design
Creative Director: Colin Baden
Art Director: Rick Yamauchi,
Kevin Kwan

Designer: Brian Takumi
Illustrator: Brian Takumi
Photographer: Craig Saruwatari
Client: Oakely Inc

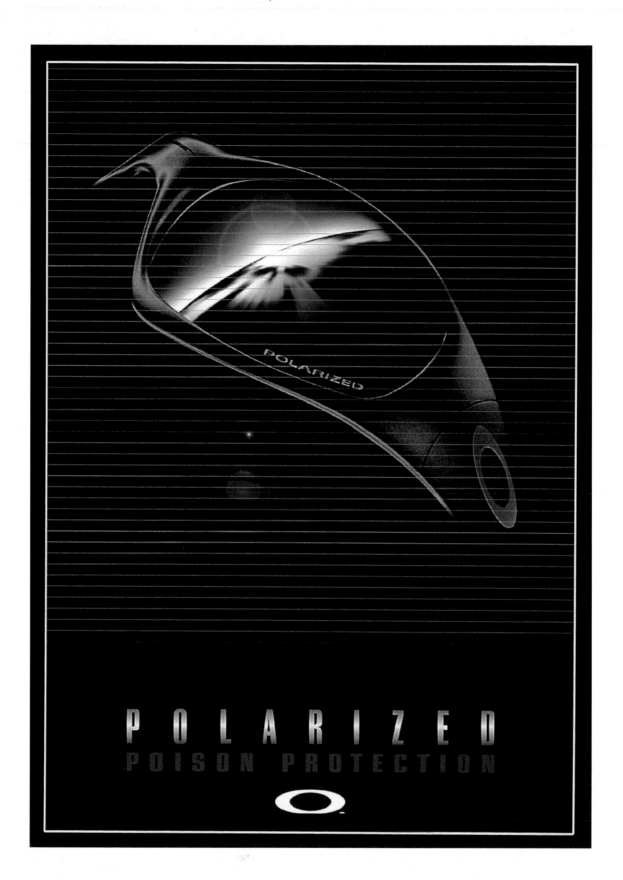

(This spread)
Design Firm: Turner Duckworth
Creative Director: David Turner, Bruce Duckworth
Designer: Allen Raulet, Johnathan Warner
Phtotographer: Lloyd Hryciw
Client: Nike

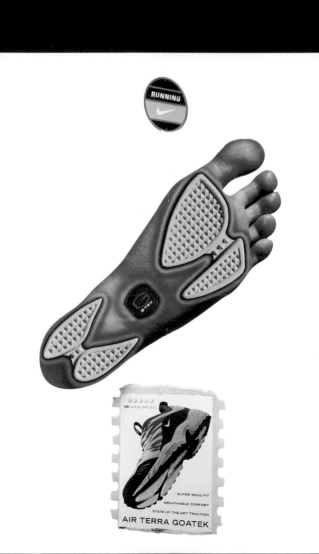

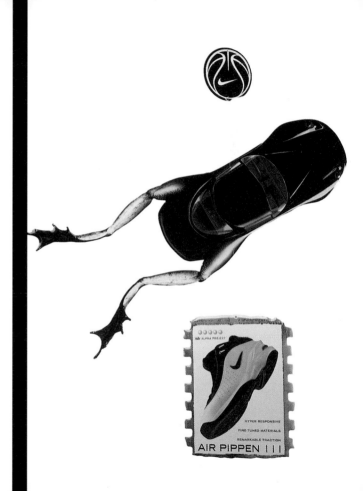

RADICAL OUTSOLE DESIGN
PHENOMENAL PROTECTION
SEAMLESS CONSTRUCTION

AIR MAX 120

HYPER RESPONSIVE
FINE-TUNED MATERIALS
REMARKABLE TRACTION

AIR PIPPEN III

Crate&Barrel

Mammea americana excelsa

mother's day
arrangements

Crate&Barrel

mother's day
arrangements

Papaver hurricanis decoratus

Crate&Barrel

mother's day
arrangements

tulipa teufotaler giganteum

Crate&Barrel

mother's day
arrangements

Vindifolius dicholor

(This spread)
Design Firm: Tapia–Tucker
Creative Director: Jose Tapia,
Michele Tucker
Art Director: Jose Tapia
Writer: Michele Tucker
Photographer: Francois Robert
Client: Crate & Barrel

Crate&Barrel

mother's day
arrangements

Millefoliatus azureus swirleus

PENALTY #17

DON'T WATCH FOOTBALL?

YOUR CALL BUTTON HAS BEEN TEMPORARILY DISCONNECTED.

Southwest Airlines • Proud sponsor of the 🏈NFL

PENALTY #32

WE HEARD YOU'RE NOT A FOOTBALL FAN.

NO PEANUTS FOR YOU.

Southwest Airlines • Proud sponsor of the 🏈NFL

WATER MAY BE THE SOURCE
OF ALL LIFE BUT YOU'RE STILL
REQUIRED TO SIGN A WAIVER.

THERE'S A REASON
LIFE JACKETS
ARE ORANGE.
IT MAKES IT
A LOT EASIER
TO FIND THE BODIES.

NANTAHALA
WHITEWATER
1-800-232-7238

(This page)
Design Firm: Oakley Design
Creative Director: Colin Baden
Art Director: Rick Yamauchi
Designer: Kevin Kwan
Photographer: Michael Yoorhees
Client: Oakely Sunglasses

(Opposite page)
Design Firm: Vanderbyl Design
Creative Director, Art Director,
Designer: Michael Vanderbyl
Client: America One

SPIRIT

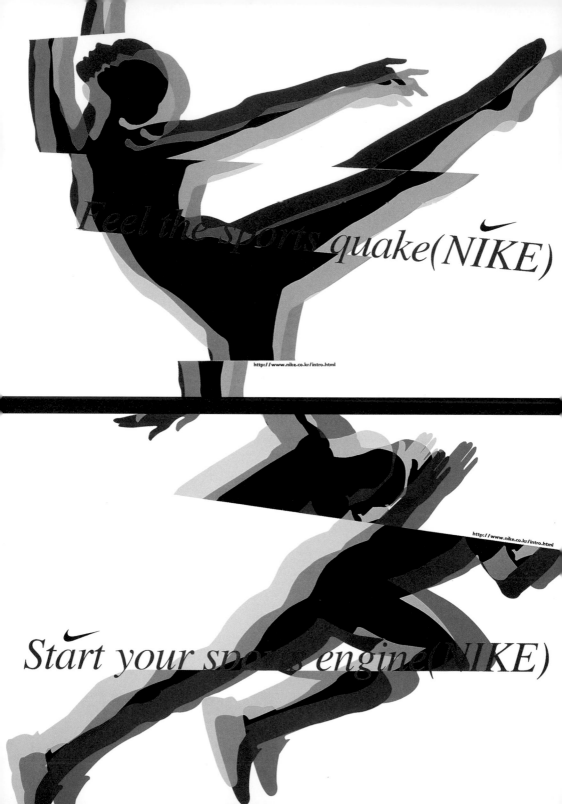

(This page)
Design Firm: William Eisner
& Association
Art Director: Scott Conklin
Writer: Scott Lynch
Photographer: Dave Gilo
Client: Wiebe Music, Chicago

(Opposite page)
Creative Director: Kum Jun Park
Art Director: Jong In Jung
Designer: Jong In Jung, Jong Pil Lee
Writer: Joon Young Bae
Illustrator: Han Kim
Client: Nike

(This page)
Design Firm: Luba Lukova Studio
Designer: Luba Lukova
Illustrator: Luba Lukova

Client: Columbia University
Theatre Division

(This page)
Design Firm: Luba Lukova Studio
Designer: Luba Lukova
Illustrator: Luba Lukova

Client: Columbia University
Theatre Division

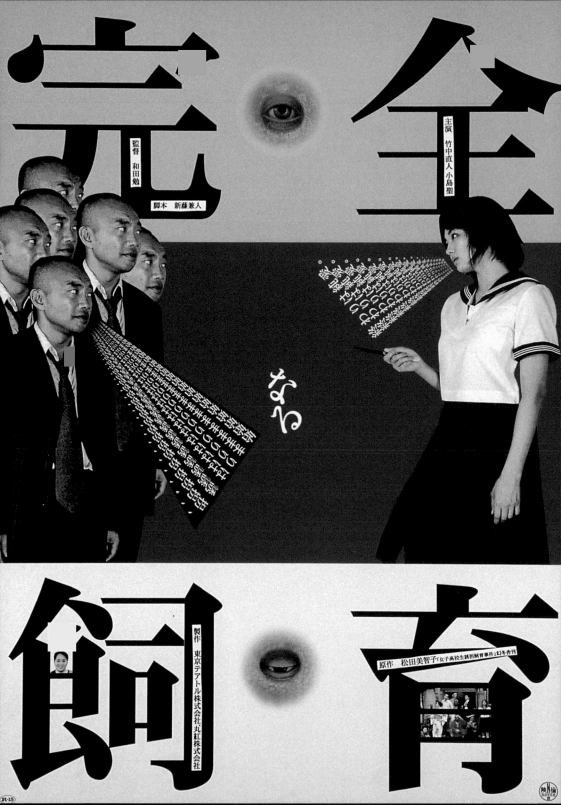

完全なる飼育

(This page)
Creative Director, Art Director,
Designer: Tadanori Yokoo
Writer: Junko Narusawa

Photographer: Mitsuru Tabei
Client: Marubeni Corporation
Tokyo Theatres Co

(This page)
Design Firm: Just Partners
Creative Director: Carolyn McGeorge
Art Director: Chris Just, Mark Brady
Writer: Mark Brady, Chris Just
Illustrator: Jeff Satterthwaite
Client: Richmond Symphony

(Opposite page)
Design Firm: Spot Design
Creative Director: Drew Hodges
Designer: Kristina Decorpo
Writer: Tom Greenwald
Illustrato: Mart Stutzman
Client: National Artist
Management Company

Bernadette Peters
in Irving Berlin's
Annie Get Your Gun

ALSO STARRING
TOM WOPAT

HIS TARGETS KISSED BY KNIVES BUT NEVER CUT!

TOMMY KEELER

EVERY BULLET A BULLSEYE!

FRANK BUTLER

COWBOY, SHOWMAN, LEGEND!

BOSTON
SEATTLE
CHICAGO
WASHINGTON DC

BUFFALO BILL

AS LOVELY AS THEY ARE FEARLESS!

TATE SISTERS

AMAZING **ANNIE OAKLEY**
FROM BACKWOODS GIRL TO SHOOTIN' STAR!

(This page)
Design Firm: Cyclone
Designers: Dennis Clouse, Traci
Daberko
Illustrators: Dennis Clouse,
Traci Daberko
Client: Intiman Theatre

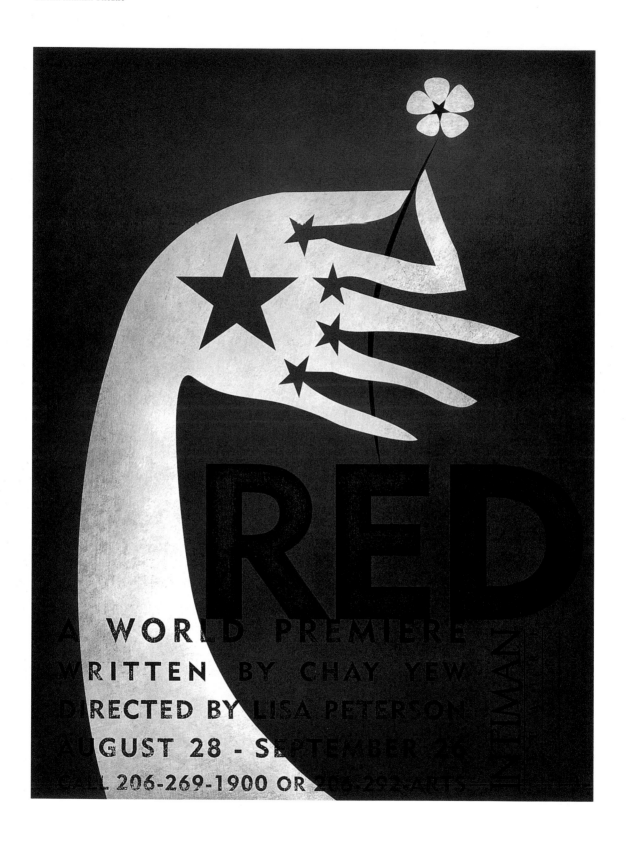

RED
A WORLD PREMIERE
WRITTEN BY CHAY YEW
DIRECTED BY LISA PETERSON
AUGUST 28 - SEPTEMBER 26
CALL 206-269-1900 OR 206-292-ARTS

(Opposite page)
Design Firm: HKGD
Creative Director, Art Director,
Designer: Henrik Kubel
Client: Barbican Centre

Victory over the sun

Alexey Kruchonykh

18 June at 8pm
19 June at 5pm & 8pm
20 June at 4pm
1999

There will be a post show talk led
by Julia Hollander on Saturday the
19th of June at 6pm

THE PIT
Barbican Centre
London EC2Y 8DS

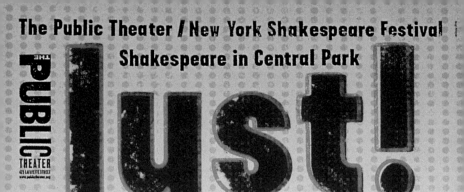

The Public Theater / New York Shakespeare Festival
Shakespeare in Central Park

THE PUBLIC THEATER
475 LAFAYETTE STREET
www.publictheater.org

lust!
(In Central Park)

Written by William Shakespeare Directed by Mel Shapiro

The Taming of the

[June 17 / July 11]

Shrew

George C.
Wolfe,
Producer

[August 10 / September 5]

and

Tartuffe

Written by Molière Directed by Mark Brokaw
English verse translation by Richard Wilbur

Ticket Policy

Pick up your free tickets on the
day of the performance begin-
ning at 1PM at the Delacorte in
Central Park, or from 1 to 3PM at
The Public Theater. This summer,
we will again distribute tickets
in each of the five boroughs on
selected dates. For more information call 212.539.8750

Tuesday through Sunday evenings at
3PM

[Delacorte Theater entrances
Central Park West at 81st Street
5th Avenue at 79th Street]

Shakespeare in Central Park is presented with the
cooperation of the City of New York, Rudolph W. Giuliani,
Mayor; The City Council, Peter F. Vallone, Speaker; Department
of Cultural Affairs, Schuyler Chapin, Commissioner; Department of Parks and Recreation, Henry J. Stern, Commissioner

(This page)
Design Firm: Spot Design
Creative Director: Drew Hodges
Designer: Lia Chee
Photographer: Lorenzo Agius
Client: Schubert Organization

(Opposite page)
Design Firm: Pentagram Design Inc
Art Director: Paula Scher
Designer: Tina Chang
Client: Public Theatre New York

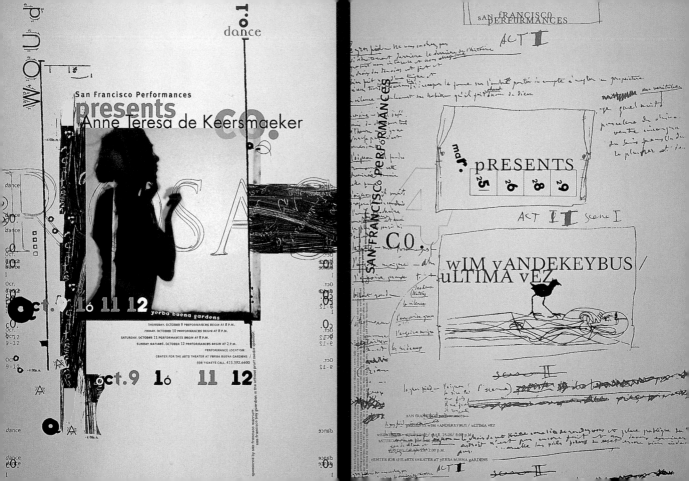

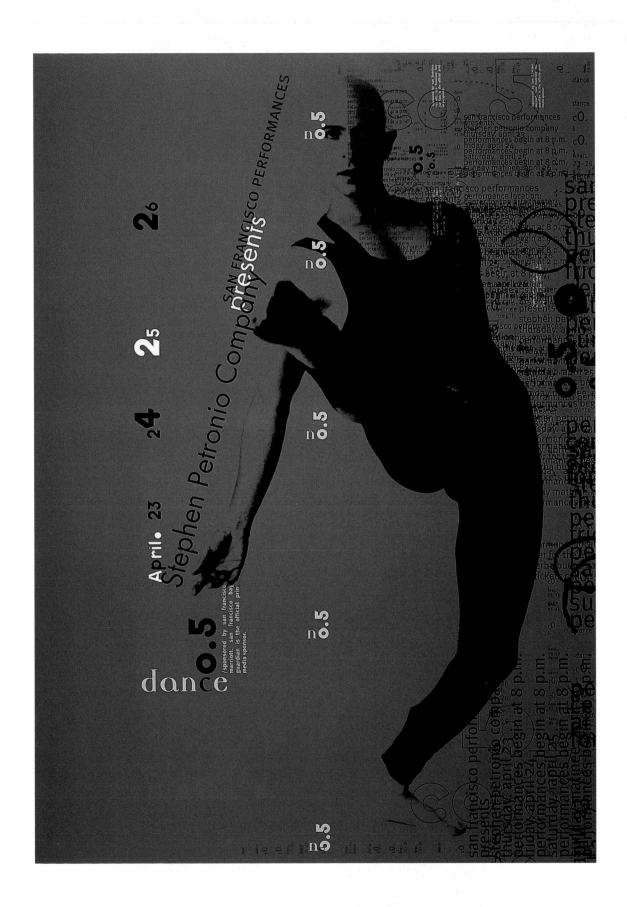

(This spread)
Design Firm: K.D. Geissbuhler
Creative Director, Art Director,
Designer: K.D. Geissbuhler
Writer: K.D. Geissbuhler

Illustrator: K.D. Geissbuhler
Photographer: K.D. Geissbuhler
Client: Opera House Zurich

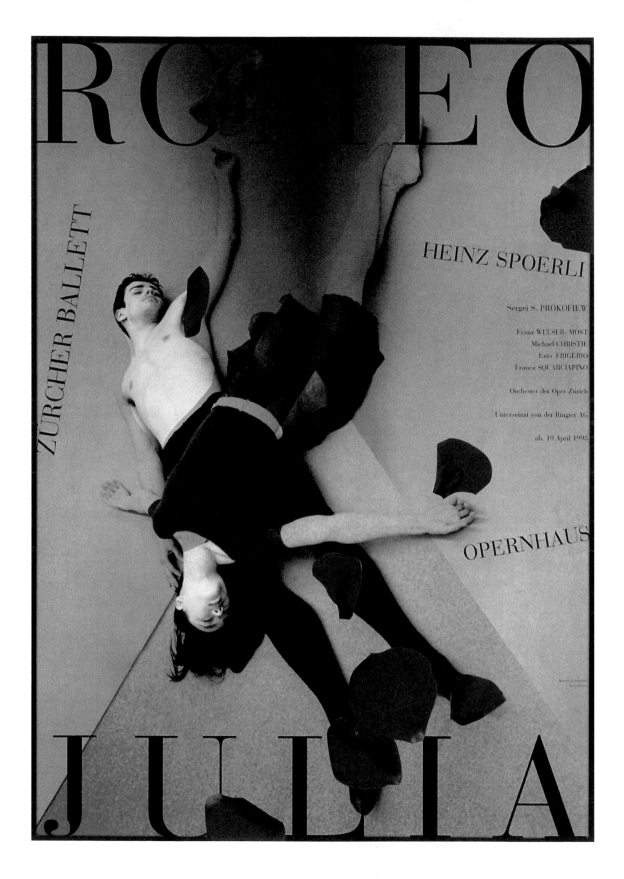

(This page)
Design Firm: Cyclone
Designer: Dennis Clouse, Traci Daberko
Photographer: Nick Vaccaro
Client: Intiman Theatre

GROSS
INDECENCY
THE THREE TRIALS
OF OSCAR WILDE
1998 OUTER CRITICS AWARD:
"BEST OFF-BROADWAY PLAY"
WRITTEN BY MOISÉS KAUFMAN
INTIMAN
THEATRE
DIRECTED BY VICTOR PAPPAS
WARNER SHOOK·ARTISTIC DIRECTOR
JUNE 4 - JULY 5 · 269-1900 OR 292-ARTS

(Opposite page)
Creative Director, Art Director,
Designer: Tadanori Yokoo
Photographer: Kazumi Kurigami
Client: Shochiku Co Ltd

(This page)
Design Firm: Loeffler Ketchum
Mountjoy
Creative Director: Jim Mountjoy
Art Director: Doug Pederson
Photographer: Jim Arndt
Writer: Curtis Smith
Client: Biltmore Estate

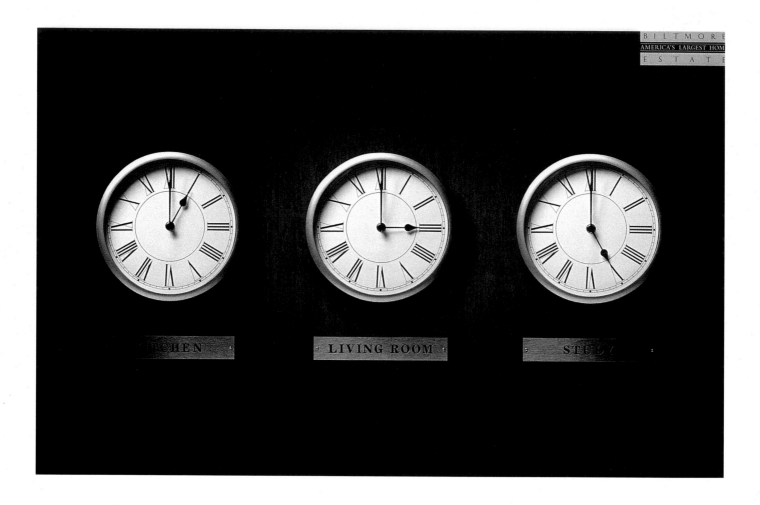

(Opposite page)
Design Firm: Pinkhaus
Creative Director: Joel Fuller
Art Director, Designer: Todd Houser
Writer: Doug Poley
Photographer: Michael Dakota
Client: Swept Away Resort

(Next page)
Creative Director: Rich Silverstein
Art Director: Jamie Spittler
Designer: Michael Schwab
Illustrator: Michael Schwab
Client: Golden Gate National
Parks Association

away   *away*   *away*

totally   *swept*

away

Swept Away
Negril Jamaica

SUTRO HEIGHTS

PhotographersIllustrators

Firms

Clients

CreativeDirectorsArtDirectorDesigners

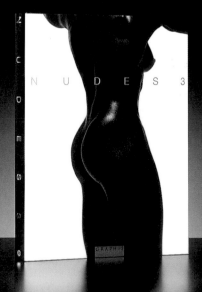

GRAPHIS
Design Annual 2000

GRAPHIS
Photo Annual 2000

GRAPHIS
New Talent Design Annual 1999

"One of the great
achievements in a
professional's career
is to have their
work reproduced in
Graphis. The greater
achievement is to
do it as a student."

Kazumasa Nagai
Geof Kern
Del Terrelonge
Gavino Sanna
Cahan & Associates
Matthew Carter

!

GRAPHIS
DesignAgencies.Com

NUDES3

GRAPHIS

GRAPHIS

GRAPHIS
Advertising Annual 2000

Order Form

We're introducing a great way to reward *Graphis* magazine readers: If you subscribe to *Graphis*, you'll qualify for a 40% discount on our books. If you subscribe and place a Standing Order, you'll get a 50% discount on our books. A Standing Order means we'll reserve your selected Graphis Annual or Series title(s) at press and ship it to you at 50% discount. With a Standing Order for *Design Annual 1999*, for example, you'll receive this title at half-off, and each coming year, we'll send you the newest *Design Annual* at this low price— an ideal way for the professional to keep informed, year after year. In addition to the titles here, we carry books in all communication disciplines, so call if there's another title we can get for you. Thank you for supporting Graphis.

Book title	Order No.	Retail	40% off Discount	Standing Order 50% off	Quantity	Totals	Call for Entries
Advertising Annual 1999	1500	☐ $70.00	☐ $42.00	☐ $35.00			
Annual Reports 6 (s)	1550	☐ $70.00	☐ $42.00	☐ $35.00			
Apple Design	1259	☐ $45.00	☐ $27.00	N/A			
Black & White Blues	4710	☐ $40.00	☐ $24.00	N/A			
Book Design 2 (s)	1453	☐ $70.00	☐ $42.00	☐ $35.00			
Brochures 3 (s)	1496	☐ $70.00	☐ $42.00	☐ $35.00			
Corporate Identity 3 (s)	1437	☐ $70.00	☐ $42.00	☐ $35.00			
Digital Photo 1 (s)	1593	☐ $70.00	☐ $42.00	☐ $35.00			
Ferenc Berko	1445	☐ $60.00	☐ $36.00	N/A			
Information Architects	1380	☐ $35.00	☐ $21.00	N/A			
Interactive Design 1 (s)	1631	☐ $70.00	☐ $42.00	☐ $35.00			
Letterhead 4 (s)	1577	☐ $70.00	☐ $42.00	☐ $35.00			
Logo Design 4 (s)	1585	☐ $60.00	☐ $36.00	☐ $30.00			
New Talent Design Annual 1999	1607	☐ $60.00	☐ $36.00	☐ $30.00			
Nudes 1	212	☐ $50.00	☐ $30.00	N/A			
Photo Annual 1998	1461	☐ $70.00	☐ $42.00	☐ $35.00			
Pool Light	1470	☐ $70.00	☐ $42.00	N/A			
Poster Annual 1999	1623	☐ $70.00	☐ $42.00	☐ $35.00			
Product Design 2 (s)	1330	☐ $70.00	☐ $42.00	☐ $35.00			
Promotion Design 1 (s)	1615	☐ $70.00	☐ $42.00	☐ $35.00			
T-Shirt Design 2 (s)	1402	☐ $60.00	☐ $36.00	☐ $30.00			
Typography 2	1267	☐ $70.00	☐ $42.00	☐ $35.00			
Walter Iooss	1569	☐ $60.00	☐ $36.00	N/A			
World Trademarks	1070	☐ $250.00	☐ $150.00	N/A			
Shipping & handling per book, US $7.00, Canada $15.00, International $20.00.							N/A
New York State shipments add 8.25% tax.							N/A

Standing Orders I understand I am committing to the selected annuals and/or series and will be automatically charged for each new volume in forthcoming years, at 50% off. I must call and cancel my order when I am no longer interested in purchasing the book. (To honor your Standing Order discount you must sign below.)

Signature _____ Date _____

Calls For Entry

If you would like to receive a call for entry for any of the annuals or series please check the appropriate box, in the last column above. You can also find contest information on the Graphis website:

www.graphis.com

Graphis magazine				
	☐ One year subscription	USA $90	Canada $125	Int'l $125
	☐ Two year subscription	USA $165	Canada $235	Int'l $235
	☐ One year student*	USA $65	Canada $90	Int'l $90
	☐ Single or Back Issues (per)	USA $24	Canada $28	Int'l $28

*All students must mail a copy of student ID along with the order form.

(s) = series (published every 2-4 years)

Name	☐ American Express ☐ Visa ☐ Mastercard ☐ Check
Company	
Address	Card #
City State Zip	Expiration
Daytime phone	Card holder's signature

Send this order form (or copy) and make check payable to Graphis Inc. For even faster turn-around service, or if you have any questions about subscribing, contact us at the following numbers: in the US (800) 209.4234; outside the US (212) 532. 9387 ext. 242 or 240; fax (212) 696.4242. Check for our mailing address or order Graphis anywhere in the world at www.graphis.com

Order Graphis on the Web from anywhere in the world: www.graphis.com